DEVELOPING EMOTIONAL RESILIENCE

	Essentials	Skills	Results
PERSONAL RESILIENCE Handling your emotions	**Self-worth** Feelings about yourself and how you function at work. **Self-control** Keeping your feelings under control in response to everyday work events. **Mood** Your emotional state in any given moment.	**Shifting** Changing your emotional state in response to everyday events. **Problem solving** Resolving problems of a personal, emotional or interpersonal nature by tuning into emotions as data.	**Energy** Sustaining your strength and vitality to perform at your best. **Thriving** Organising yourself to be effective under pressure.
TEAM RESILIENCE Handling emotions in interactions with others	**Empathy** Tuning into other people's feelings so that you can take them on board when making decisions. **Understanding** Tuning into what colleagues need in order for them to be effective at work. **Caring** Showing that other people matter so that colleagues are able to make their best effort at work.	**Expressing** Communicating your feelings and thoughts to others at work. **Group empathy** Tuning into and shifting emotions at group level to stay on track with your work goals. **Dialogue** Discussing feelings when there is a problem.	**Connection** Building relationships through _____ interactions. **Influence** Leading and man___ with stakeholders members.

Praise for *Emotional Resilience*

'At last, an accessible book with practical, clear steps on how to improve this essential attribute for high performance.'

Adrian Rycroft, Former Head of
Royal Air Force Human Performance Centre

'An invaluable guide to learn to recognise and control emotions to achieve the best at work and in life.'

Attilio Pisoni, President,
Schlumberger Italiana S.p.A.

'A fantastic toolkit, which the reader can dip into to address so many different everyday challenges.'

Steve Langhorn, Director,
Rentokil Initial Sales Faculty

'This excellent and practical book on emotional resilience and how it affects your business should be a must for every manager and leader.'

Olaf Dünnweller, Senior Sales Manager,
Symantec (Deutschland) GmbH

'A powerful book showing how to achieve your best at work and enjoy doing it!'

Matthew Price, Chief Financial Officer,
MoneySuperMarket.com

'A remarkably easy, yet brilliant, read! A must-have guide for anyone who wants the edge on effectively managing themselves and other people.'

Mel Ramsey, Chief Executive Officer,
New Century Care

Emotional Resilience

7th Oct 2015
Paris

PEARSON

At Pearson, we believe in learning – all kinds of learning for all kinds of people. Whether it's at home, in the classroom or in the workplace, learning is the key to improving our life chances.

That's why we're working with leading authors to bring you the latest thinking and best practices, so you can get better at the things that are important to you. You can learn on the page or on the move, and with content that's always crafted to help you understand quickly and apply what you've learned.

If you want to upgrade your personal skills or accelerate your career, become a more effective leader or more powerful communicator, discover new opportunities or simply find more inspiration, we can help you make progress in your work and life.

Pearson is the world's leading learning company. Our portfolio includes the Financial Times and our education business, Pearson International.

Every day our work helps learning flourish, and wherever learning flourishes, so do people.

To learn more, please visit us at **www.pearson.com/uk**

Emotional Resilience

Know what it takes to be agile, adaptable and perform at your best

Geetu Bharwaney

Harlow, England • London • New York • Boston • San Francisco • Toronto • Sydney
Auckland • Singapore • Hong Kong • Tokyo • Seoul • Taipei • New Delhi
Cape Town • São Paulo • Mexico City • Madrid • Amsterdam • Munich • Paris • Milan

PEARSON EDUCATION LIMITED
Edinburgh Gate
Harlow CM20 2JE
United Kingdom
Tel: +44 (0)1279 623623
Web: www.pearson.com/uk

First published 2015 (print and electronic)

Pearson Education is not responsible for the content of third-party internet sites.

ISBN: 978-1-292-07366-8 (print)
      978-1-292-07368-2 (PDF)
      978-1-292-07369-9 (ePub)
      978-1-292-07367-5 (eText)

British Library Cataloguing-in-Publication Data
A catalogue record for the print edition is available from the British Library

Library of Congress Cataloging-in-Publication Data
Bharwaney, Geetu.
   Emotional resilience : know what it takes to be agile, adaptable and perform at your best / Geetu Bharwaney.
      pages cm
   Includes bibliographical references and index.
   ISBN 978-1-292-07366-8
   1. Emotional intelligence. 2. Resilience (Personality trait) 3. Performance. I. Title.
   BF576.B43 2014
   152.4--dc23

                          2015003620

10 9 8 7 6 5 4 3 2 1
19 18 17 16 15

Text design and illustrations by Design Deluxe
Cover design by Rob Day
Cover image © Africa Studio, Shuttlestock

Print edition typeset in 9.5/13pt Mundo Sans by 3
Printed in Great Britain by Henry Ling Ltd, at the Dorset Press, Dorchester, Dorset

NOTE THAT ANY PAGE CROSS REFERENCES REFER TO THE PRINT EDITION

Dedication

To my dad for all you have taught me and provided for me.

Thank you for supporting me through every step and valuable learning experience.

Your deep knowledge and wisdom remain with me forever.

'The unexamined life is not worth living.'

SOCRATES, ANCIENT GREEK PHILOSOPHER

CONTENTS

FOREWORD

All organisations rely upon the effectiveness of the people within them – their individual effectiveness and their effectiveness in teams. This is true for businesses, governments, academic institutions and charities. I have pursued a career in business, and I see this truth whatever the nature of the company may be. Capital intensive businesses, like those in energy and mining, still need the people driving performance to be very effective, otherwise all that capital will be wasted. People-intensive businesses, for instance retailing and professional services, cannot operate without their raw material, their people, being truly productive and effective.

Given this, bookstores are full of books about how organisations can be most effective. The themes of 'leadership', 'teamwork' and 'performance' are to be found in title after title. Many of these books provide good tactical and practical advice. 'Resilience' has become a theme of much writing about organisations. This should be no surprise. Given the pace of change in the world economy, the result of globalisation and the emergence of new technologies, companies are faced with the need to evolve and change – transformation has become a constant for many organisations.

What distinguishes the work of Geetu Bharwaney is that it is based both upon a firm intellectual basis, over 15 years of work in the field of emotional intelligence, and 25 years of practical work as a coach and mentor to individuals and organisations. I have seen Geetu's work at first hand, and how it can make a real difference to the effectiveness of organis-ations. In her work, Geetu recognises that without emotion there can be no lasting motivation, and without motivation there can be no energy in an organisation. Emotional balance and resilience, indeed happiness, go hand in hand with individual and team performance. This focus on driving performance, through understanding the essentials that underpin individual and team performance and building the skills to unlock organisational energy, is a characteristic of Geetu's work.

Emotional Resilience therefore is both very relevant, while also having strong foundations, being the result of both academic research and years of practical work and refinement. Within this book, readers will find a coherent framework for thinking through how to increase individual and team effectiveness through resilience, and great practical advice and actions to turn this framework into reality.

Dominic Casserley
Chief Executive Officer
Willis Group Holdings plc

ABOUT THE AUTHOR

Geetu Bharwaney is the Founding Director of Ei World Limited, a company at the forefront of globally advancing innovative development programmes. Geetu is widely recognised as a pioneer practitioner in delivering talent management, leadership development, team effectiveness and CEO coaching based on emotional intelligence and emotional resilience.

She has delivered programmes on emotional resilience in 37 countries since 1999 and is the longest established coach specialising in emotional intelligence in the UK.

Geetu is available to support talent and organisational development of the world's best companies. She speaks regularly at conferences and corporate events and is a member of the EI Consortium, set up to promote the value, applied research and application of emotional intelligence in organisations.

Ei World has a strategic alliance with AIIR Consulting for the delivery of coaching on demand, any time anywhere.

Geetu Bharwaney
E: gbharwaney@eiworld.org
All web resources at: **eiworld.org/emotionalresilience**

ACKNOWLEDGEMENTS

I would like to thank Dominic Casserley for writing the foreword of this book. Your personal understanding of the relevance of emotional resilience in business is both inspiring and deeply appreciated.

I would also like to thank Eloise Cook from Pearson without whom the idea for this book would have remained just an idea. You have been an ideal partner to bring this book to fruition.

To my partner Mark, thank you for supporting me through each step of the journey.

Experts

I am grateful to my teachers on emotion. You have helped me to understand the role of emotion in individual and team resilience. Most importantly, you inspired me in your own way to communicate globally the value of emotional resilience and to make this topic accessible to people at work everywhere.

Thank you to all members of the Consortium for Research on Emotional Intelligence in Organisations (CREIO). You have introduced me to a myriad of concepts of emotional intelligence and inspired me to keep developing as a practitioner in the field.

Barbara Sorenson – emotional and family health

Professor Vanessa Urch Druskat and Dr Steven B. Wolff – team emotional intelligence

ACKNOWLEDGEMENTS

Dr Konstantin Vassilis Petrides – trait emotional intelligence

Dr Jonathan Kirschner - business psychology

Harold Klemp – spiritual teachings of Eckankar

Dr Mark Atkinson – the importance of emotional health

Colleagues and friends

A special thank you to my support system of colleagues at Ei World, AIIR Consulting and friends who provided critical feedback, praise and helpful suggestions within my deadlines. Thank you for contributions to making this book better:

Adèle MacKinlay, Alison Baugh, Carmel Lewis, Gemma Prichard, Helen Lappert, Dr Jonathan Kirschner, Katherine Baldwin, Nasreen Memon, Neel Kamal, Eike Marx and Dr Yomi Ajayi-obe.

Clients

And finally, thank you to all clients and strategic partners of Ei World who continue to experiment with and have courage to test out the tools and tips in this book to face the everyday work challenges in your arenas of work, you are too numerous to mention...

Publisher's acknowledgements

The publishers are grateful to the following for permission to reproduce copyright material:

Hachette Book Group and Profile Books for permission to reproduce the list of annoying habits of leaders in Marshall Goldsmith (2008) *What Got You Here Won't Get You There*. London: Profile Books. Used by permission of Hachette Books and Profile Books.

In some instances we have been unable to trace the owners of copyright material and we would appreciate any information that would enable us to do so.

INTRODUCTION

> 'Resilience is now recognised as an important factor in the workplace. In the (...) turbulent context of today's working world, the resilience of both individuals and organisations becomes paramount in order to survive and thrive.'
>
> **CHARTERED INSTITUTE FOR PERSONNEL AND DEVELOPMENT,** *DEVELOPING RESILIENCE: AN EVIDENCE-BASED GUIDE FOR PRACTITIONERS* (2011) P. 2

This book provides a method for achieving personal and team resilience. I want to start by explaining where these ideas come from.

My perspectives on emotional resilience have emerged from 25 years as a coach and facilitator, helping clients improve their effectiveness and performance at work. Over the last 16 years, I have specialised in the concept of emotional intelligence, as I started to recognise that emotion is what people struggle with on a daily basis. For most people, it is not technical skills or knowledge that is the gap between where they are and where they want to be in terms of their performance at work. It is the understanding of how emotion in us and others affects everything we think and do. Many people fail to understand the root of problems at work and difficulties under pressure, so they do not fix their problems for the long term. As a direct consequence, they end up not performing at their best. In situations at work, by not taking emotion into account (their own and other people's), what happens is that often they end up not fulfilling their potential but working below it. Some will end up unwell and unable to work at all. My belief is that this can be avoided through paying attention to emotion.

Emotional Resilience

EMOTIONAL RESILIENCE IS...

choosing the thoughts, actions and feelings that enable us to perform at our best.

'Where there is emotion, there is a need for emotional resilience.'

WHY EMOTIONAL RESILIENCE?

Emotions...

→ affect WHAT we do and HOW we do it.

→ matter for success, work productivity, health, personal effectiveness and team performance.

→ play a role in how we think and behave.

→ are continuous and automatic; we can't stop them from coming whether or not we are aware of them.

'Technical skills are no longer enough, human skills make the difference.' **People struggle with emotion. This book shows you what to do.**

You will:

→ learn more about yourself (it's SELF-REVEALING);

→ **know what to do differently to achieve high performance and set yourself up for success (it's COMPREHENSIVE);**

→ consider emotions more concretely in everyday life (it's PRACTICAL).

What's in it for you?

→ Learn to be more effective at work.
→ Be able to handle situations better.
→ Overcome obstacles more easily.
→ Better control of your feelings, actions and thoughts.
→ Sustain performance at a high level.
→ Improve your relationships.

Three central concerns that everyone has...

❶ How do I solve everyday problems involving people?
❷ How do I have impact / influence on my bosses and stakeholders?
❸ How do I achieve what I want?

Author's experience based on:

→ 25 years' coaching
→ 15,000 clients
→ 40 countries

ROLE OF EMOTIONS...

→ Internal assessment of what is happening to us.
→ Improves decisions if we can understand the information they provide.
→ Motivates us to address the most pressing issues in our lives.

'We are human beings not human doings.'

DARWIN QUOTE...

'It is not the strongest of the species that survives, nor the most intelligent. It is the one that is the most adaptable to change.'

'The emotional resilience framework provides the foundation for human adaptability and agility.'

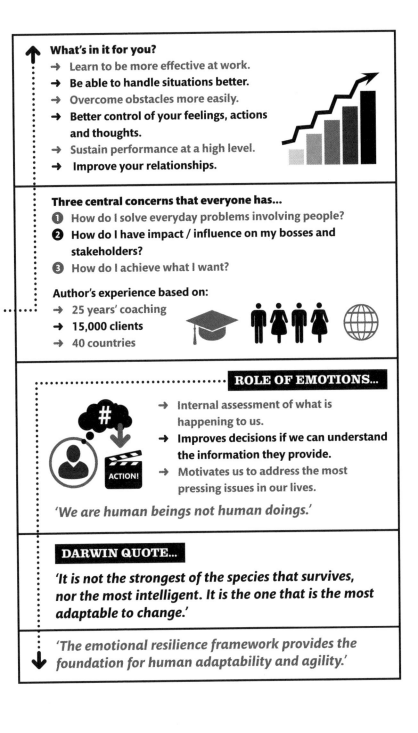

My work and perspective has been informed by client projects all over the world. I have had a privileged insight into what happens in work life every day in organisations across a full range of sizes and types of company. The everyday struggles behind business delivery and a focus on business targets include inner self-confidence, relationship problems between bosses and colleagues, and unexpected changes, which have to be dealt with. The issues that people face at work seem to be similar, no matter the sector, job or size of organisation. I used to consider executives as having unique development needs until I started to help boards of directors. I now realise that people at all levels seem to be preoccupied with the same questions – How do I solve the problems I have with people I interact with at work? How do I do my job so that it has impact/broader influence on my bosses or stakeholders? How do I operate with maximum ease so that I achieve what I want and do my best, yet still have time for other interests and priorities in my life?

This book provides a comprehensive way to build an understanding of emotion at work so that anyone can sustain high performance through personal and team resilience. The practical ideas presented here are drawn directly from exercises I use as a coach, which are proven to be effective for sustaining solutions to everyday problems. The text is designed to set you up for success in the 21st century workplace.

This book provides practical steps for learning how to handle and master emotions so that you can be emotionally resilient. I consider it a form of human upgrade on what you already know. It is a call to action to honour your own emotions and those of the people with whom you work.

Whatever your job or your ambition, learning about emotional resilience can assist you. You will be introduced to an holistic method for achieving success. I propose that emotion provides information. Understanding, managing, and making full use of emotions and the insight they provide is at the heart of personal and team resilience.

I hope you enjoy it.

What role do emotions play at work?

Emotions play a very important role in how we think and behave. Everyone is in a continuous flow of emotions, thoughts, actions and reactions in everyday work life.

Usually there are three parts to an emotion – there is the subjective part of **how we experience the emotion** (for example, I am feeling happy); a physiological part of **how our bodies react to the emotion** (for example, my body feels light when I feel happy); and a part that involves **how we behave in response to the feeling** (for example, I feel like talking to people I don't know well when I feel happy). The topic of emotional intelligence is linked to this understanding so we can start to be intelligent about our emotional responses.

Anyone who thinks that we can expect people to leave their emotions at the door each day when they arrive at work should rethink this belief. This view is outdated, unrealistic and narrow-minded. Firstly, without emotion there is no motivation. Motivation requires emotion. Secondly, human beings are not programmable robots. We are human beings not human doings. Missing this fact can lead you to ignore information that is at the heart of high performance.

All human interactions involve an exchange of emotion. You need to be able to communicate well with customers and colleagues, whatever their function or level, and this means understanding emotion. No matter how advanced technology becomes, the way we interact with others at work will always be at the heart of success or failure. Each and every interaction generates emotion.

Your emotions at work affect both what you do and how you do it. Your emotions provide you with an internal assessment about what is happening, they send you signals about problems and pleasures. Emotions are continuous and automatic, they do not stop coming whether or not you are aware of them from moment to moment. Understanding the information your emotions send and then using this to guide your thinking and actions brings you greater awareness and effectiveness.

When emotions are recognised and the information they provide is understood, they improve decisions and enable you to get the best results, not only for you, but also for others. Emotions are intended to move us (Elfenbein, 2007). They motivate us to address the most pressing issues in our lives (Ekman, 2003, p. xv).

One complication here is that most of our emotional wiring was installed at a very young age. For example, the development of trust or mistrust is thought to happen very early in life between birth and 12 months and is related largely to the quality and reliability of caregivers. *Hope* is the basic virtue that we build at this stage of development (Erickson, 1950).

Ignoring emotion means that we miss essential information in the situation – our emotions, other people's emotions and the emotions that we need to pay attention to in the situation, in order to get results.

You cannot afford to leave your emotions at the door of your workplace. By managing your emotions at work, in your ever-more-demanding workplace where your emotions matter to your everyday effectiveness, emotional resilience is more important than ever before.

What is emotional resilience?

Resilience is the capacity to survive pressured situations and to bounce back after setbacks. Very few people would dispute the importance of resilience for being successful in today's workplace.

The complication is that where there are people working together, there is *emotion*.

The practice of *emotional intelligence is* focused on recognising emotion in oneself and others, and using this awareness to connect well with others, manage stress and to make sound decisions.

However where there is emotion, I believe that there is a need to pay *continuous* attention to *emotions* both for one's own success and the success of the organisation or business enterprise.

To practise this continuous attention requires a focus on *emotional resilience* which goes beyond both resilience and emotional intelligence as we have understood them until now.

Emotional resilience includes a range of competences, skills and abilities that enable us to be effective in today's workplace. I define emotional resilience as:

the ability to continually choose the feelings, thoughts and actions that help you achieve results and perform at your best at personal, team and organisational levels.

This is *continual* because it doesn't stop after one event or one well-handled situation. No-one can say that they have *arrived* at being emotionally resilient.

To succeed at work today, we need to *sustain* success through an ongoing display of these abilities, so that we are able to perform at our best not just in the current role but in all roles we take on.

Emotional resilience includes *personal, team and organisational levels* because it affects how you feel about work, how your team gets its work done and, ultimately, how your organisation functions as a whole.

The emphasis is on knowing *how to take action* to meet your needs, the needs of others and the demands of the situation, so that you function at your best.

In this book you will learn a *structure* for making sense of emotion at work both personally and for your work in teams, so you can be effective in any setting. In other words, instead of focusing on one aspect of emotion, you are offered a way of being fully aware of your emotions, emotions of others in work teams, as well as the emotions that might stem from your own personality.

This learning journey may well involve taking a long hard look at yourself and then doing something different from what, typically, you do or think of doing, in order to be agile in the situations you face.

Emotional resilience requires focus; it is not a skill to be learned today and forgotten tomorrow. The process of learning involves time and thought from you the reader but, the more you do, the better will be your results. People who have invested in these skills, abilities and ways of thinking before you, take from it many benefits into their work.

My invitation to you is to learn about emotional resilience, master it and bring your full understanding of emotion to your workplace so that you can perform at your best.

This book will help you build your personal and team emotional resilience so you can set yourself up for success.

Why emotional resilience rather than resilience?

There are five key differences between resilience and emotional resilience:

1. Emotional resilience goes beyond resilience

For me, resilience is incomplete without incorporating emotion – emotional resilience is full resilience. It is comprehensive and far-reaching. Emotional resilience is an approach to performing at your best through a combination of self-understanding and action.

Resilience represents taking action without full commitment to all necessary steps – for example, learning mindfulness without fully understanding the impact of emotions on performance at work. There is also a lack of focus on self-understanding within resilience.

2. Emotional resilience is key to job performance

Resilience is, typically, considered as a nice-to-have ability, a bonus on top of technical or practical work skills at times of stress.

My experiences as a coach have led me to realise that emotional resilience is central to effectiveness at work. It is a set of skills and actions to use not only at times of stress but every day. Learning to be emotionally resilient helps us to increase productivity and performance at work.

It does this by helping us to reduce time-consuming tensions and turmoil through learning tools to overcome typical everyday problems at work. Many of our day-to-day problems at work involve emotion and most people do not have strategies for problem-solving emotions.

3. Emotional resilience is for everyday challenges

Resilience is viewed typically as the ability to bounce back from a difficult situation or an unexpected challenge. The reality is that emotions are always present both in us and in the people we are inter-acting with. Emotional resilience recognises the power of emotion to both help and hinder our attempts to face everyday challenges.

Emotional resilience focuses on helping us to thrive every day through understanding the power of emotion to help us or derail us. Resilience is usually called upon during times of extreme pressure or unexpected crises.

4. Emotional resilience helps you to understand and master your primal emotions

There are two central functions of our brains. Our lower brain scans for threats and ignites emotions to keep us safe (for example, by feeling fearful, we move away from the source of threat). The lower or instinctual part of our brain is 'on' permanently and is primal. Our higher brain engages with problem solving and rational thinking. Both are necessary to help us to survive.

The complication is that the lower brain (the limbic brain or emotion centre) is controlling us, unless we consciously take it over with the higher brain (the prefrontal cortex or rational thinking centre). Our unconscious mind is always at play and takes signals from emotion. It is ever-present.

Emotional resilience focuses on thoughts, actions and feelings and recognises the importance of being intelligent about our emotions.

Emotional resilience allows us to take control of our unconscious mind (lower brain) and to act more consciously. Emotion controls the unconscious – and the unconscious controls our resilience. Resilience tends to focus on thoughts and actions and rational decisions.

This is why there is no resilience without emotional resilience.

5. Emotional resilience is both an individual and a team sport

Resilience tends to emphasise personal skills exclusively with little focus on the interactions within a team. Concepts of resilience rely on you working on yourself, in order to cope better.

It is my view that resilience is not only about working on yourself – it is about building relationships with others. This is a key part of the emotional resilience framework outlined in this book. The framework demonstrates that good relationships contribute to personal resilience and shows us which behaviours we need to enact to build those relationships, whether with one or more people in a team or wider team.

Relationships are a very important source of connection at work. Resilience is a tool for individual effectiveness (to help build personal resilience). Emotional resilience is a tool for both personal and team performance. Through the skills of interacting with people at work, where emotion is ever present, emotional resilience helps build team resilience.

What is in it for you?

Given the importance of emotional resilience to your success at work, by reading this book you will learn how to:

- be more effective at work;

- handle situations better;

- overcome everyday hassles more easily;

- have better control of your feelings, actions and thoughts when you need to be at your most agile;

- have the energy to be fully engaged in tasks and perform at your best;

- improve your relationships in your team;

- increase your influence with colleagues and customers.

In summary, you will enjoy your work more and your work life will be easier.

Why now?

There has been a great deal of recent research into the benefits of emotional resilience, showing that:

- **emotionally resilient people are, typically, our highest performers.** They are both personally resilient and can also manage themselves and be resilient when working in teams, applicable across roles, types of organisation and sector.

- **emotionally resilient people have an advantage in the market-place.** Their skills and talents make them more likely to be visible as good colleagues, effective managers and skilled personnel. You will find it easier to be in a job that you enjoy and that plays to your strengths.

- **emotionally resilient organisations have an increasingly competitive edge.** They are well functioning organisations which are able to reach their goals.

 Should you want to find out more about the business case for emotional resilience please visit:
eiworld.org/emotionalresilience.
You will see this icon frequently in the book to signpost web resources.

Developing your emotional resilience

There are three steps in my programme to develop emotional resilience. This represents your pathway to understanding emotion at work – and provides a structure for learning emotional resilience. My framework is included on the inside of the front book cover.

Here is how it works. Emotional resilience is both a mindset and a skillset, leading to the achievement of results.

ESSENTIALS   SKILLS   RESULTS

The Essentials – at its core, emotional resilience requires attention to six aspects of emotion-related self-awareness, which I believe are at the core of your emotional resilience mindset. I recommend that you consider these six essentials as of critical relevance to your emotional resilience. Together, they influence what you think about and focus on, how you handle your emotions and the emotions of others, and how you operate when working in a team. Three of the essentials are about self and three are about working as part of a team. A team could be as few as two people. Both sides of resilience are important to achieving high performance at work.

The Skills – five emotion-related skills will help you to take appropriate action when you are feeling challenged in work situations. These practical skills, covered in Part 2, represent your emotional resilience skillset. Using them will help you to build personal and team resilience.

The Results – finally, once you have focused on the essentials and the skills of emotional resilience, you are likely to be performing well in four results areas at work. You will be able to fine-tune your emotional resilience in Part 3 by taking action in these four areas of your work.

How this book works

This three-part book provides you with tips and practical suggestions for improving your emotional resilience. By working through this book and applying the suggestions, you will improve your chances of sustaining high performance in your workplace through building personal and team emotional resilience.

I have designed each chapter with you in mind, and you will find the following key features:

What you need to know – some key facts and practical research.

Meet... – these are case studies of people who faced challenges with an aspect of emotional resilience and how they approached it.

Key theme – a key topic to focus on.

Activities – things you can do to boost your emotional resilience.

Web resources – many additional materials are available at **eiworld. org/emotionalresilience**. You will find electronic templates, individual surveys, team surveys, audio recordings, videos, checklists and references to further reading.

- **Map** – each essential has an emotional resilience map at the end of the chapter, to signpost you to other relevant chapters and to help direct your learning on priority topics.

Take note!

I suggest you find a notebook now, keep it handy and use it to make notes on a daily basis. This will assist you in building your knowledge of your emotional resilience and apply what you learn in your everyday work life.

Do as much observation and writing as possible as part of your learning.

This will enable you to take action and really will help you to become emotionally resilient more easily than reading passively.

The task of keeping a journal and writing in it every day is an effective way to start a conversation with yourself about your emotional life. This has been found to be very positive for building emotional resilience.

Once you start tuning in to emotion, you will start to notice how your experience of work changes over time. Mine certainly has!

Why am I writing this book?

The content in this book was born from my work with over 1,000 clients and over 15,000 people working in organisational teams that I have helped over the last 25 years. I have had the privilege of introducing insights on emotion to a wide variety of people across diverse non-profit, public, government and for-profit organisations. These include a range of occupations from construction workers, call centre operatives, and team leaders, to chief executives, senior leaders and chairmen across 40 countries.

My gold standard for deciding what to include in this book was based on my experiences with coaching senior executives in top companies throughout the world. Many of these people refuse to engage with 'soft' or 'fluffy' concepts; they need concrete and relevant ways to develop skills and abilities. My clients have used the ideas in this book to make a permanent shift in how they work and live. My toolkit of exercises, suggestions and tips will be helpful to you if you want to become the best version of yourself at work and in life using the power of emotions. This is what I hope will be your experience from both reading this book and doing the activities recommended. Whilst I appreciate the relevance and value of science and research, this book is an action book, something you can work through to help yourself be better equipped at work.

I have created a framework for developing emotional resilience, explaining what to do first, and how to proceed until you get the results you desire. I share the framework so that you can benefit from it and work with it systematically. This will give you a practical focus on emotion for building personal and team resilience.

Make emotional resilience a priority in your learning this year. You won't look back! Let's get started.

Start point: self-reflection

First, it is important and useful to understand how you function at work currently. Here is a self-reflection activity on the six essentials in Part 1 to define how you function naturally at work. This starting point will help you to decide the order in which to read this book. Move to learning about the skills after you have worked through the priority essentials where you have the most negative impacts.

Instructions

The purpose of this self-reflection is to help you to prioritise your reading of the chapters in this book. Each of the six aspects of self-awareness has a number of descriptions of typical thoughts, feelings and actions associated with the topic.

1. Find a time to do this reflection quietly away from others.

2. Look at the phrases and circle all those in each row that describe the way you work.

3. Do this for all five rows of descriptions, on each page.

4. Each time you reach a row titled 'Negative impact' (appears twice in each page as a shaded row), please fill in a circle on the separate worksheet 'Priority topics for emotional resilience'. This is included in the back of the book, but can also be downloaded. By noting the negative impacts of these core aspects of emotional self-awareness, you will start to develop a visible summary of you at your worst: a picture that will help you to prioritise your reading of the book.

There are further instructions at the end of the reflection activity.

Reflect on your self-worth

Here is a list of typical thoughts, feelings and actions associated with self-worth.

1. Please circle all phrases in each row that apply to the way you work.

2. Each time you circle a 'Negative impact' characteristic, please colour a circle on your 'Priority topics for emotional resilience' worksheet.

Very high	Negative impact	• I am aloof. • I do not accept feedback. • I overestimate my own level of control. • I am self-centred and ambitious with a big ego.	• I am defensive when criticised. • I am not aware of my own weaknesses. • I blame mistakes on others.
	Positive impact	• I am satisfied with life. • I feel confident. • I am energetic. • I am bold with a positive outlook.	• I expect success and get success. • I handle criticism well. • I am aware of my strengths.
Medium/ balance	Typical behaviours	• I feel good enough. • I accept that I do not have to be perfect. • I do not obsess about 100 per cent accuracy. • I am comfortable and genuine with others.	• I am open about my strengths and weaknesses. • I have occasional self-doubt though it does not get in my way. • I am reasonably self-assured.
Very low	Negative impact	• I lack confidence. • I do not inspire others. • I underestimate my own abilities. • I set low aspirations.	• I worry excessively about mistakes. • I fear failure. • I expect negative feedback.
	Positive impact	• I am modest, unpretentious and accessible to others. • I do not overestimate my own level of control. • I am considered to be a safe pair of hands. • I have a realistic view of my talents and shortcomings.	• I am open to views of others and accept criticism well. • I learn from my mistakes. • I value the team more than myself.

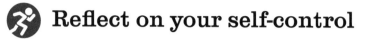

Reflect on your self-control

Here is a list of typical thoughts, feelings and actions associated with self-control.

1. Please circle all phrases in each row that apply to the way you work.

2. Each time you circle a 'Negative impact' characteristic, please colour a circle on your 'Priority topics for emotional resilience' worksheet.

Very high	Negative impact	• I am seen as too relaxed. • I am overly cautious. • I procrastinate and am slow to get started. • I take decisions slowly and avoid risk.	• I miss opportunities/deadlines. • I demotivate other colleagues through lack of action. • I am too bureaucratic/rule-bound or process-oriented.
	Positive impact	• I plan well in advance. • I remain in control at all times. • I carefully consider projects. • I exercise great care and accuracy.	• I pay attention to consequences of actions. • I use past experience and past mistakes as a guide to action. • I see the big picture.
Medium/ balanced	Typical behaviours	• I think before I act. • I rely on reasoning. • I use information to solve problems. • I make quick decisions when necessary.	• I stay in control. • I make appropriate plans. • I am tolerant of people and understanding.
Very low	Negative impact	• I tend to have a very messy workspace. • I act rashly and regret my actions. • I do not consider risks. • I do not weigh up pros and cons.	• I disregard important dates. • I make frequent mistakes from my lack of attention to detail. • I am perceived as unpredictable and impulsive with negative consequences in relationships.
	Positive impact	• I am known as someone who is passionate. • I make tough decisions. • I am comfortable solving problems. • I am at ease with challenges.	• I am spontaneous and creative. • I take advantage of opportunities. • I am flexible and can meet deadlines.

Reflect on your mood

Here is a list of typical thoughts, feelings and actions associated with mood.

1. Please circle all phrases in each row that apply to the way you work.

2. Each time you circle a 'Negative impact' characteristic, please colour a circle on your 'Priority topics for emotional resilience' worksheet.

Very high	Negative impact	• I have unrealistically positive views. • I am complacent. • I have too high expectations of self and others. • I have unrealistic career goals.	• I over promise and under deliver. • I do not recognise potential problems before they happen. • I am unwilling to learn from mistakes.
	Positive impact	• I am usually in a positive mood. • I have infectious enthusiasm, which helps motivate others. • I am very self-confident. • I am able to energise others.	• I remain in a positive mood, even when problems arise. • I can identify opportunities in problem situations. • My positive mood often leads to positive results.
Medium/ balanced	Typical behaviours	• My mood is consistent. • I am positive about the future. • I get along well with others.	• I am even-tempered. • I am not overly excitable. • I am considered to be balanced in my mood. • I am easy-going.
Very low	Negative impact	• My low mood may overlook possibilities. • Negative possibilities tend to dominate in my mind and paralyse my decision making. • I underestimate my abilities.	• I am overly sensitive to negative feedback. • I do not believe it is important to manage my mood. • My pessimism creates mistrust with colleagues. • I am downbeat more than upbeat.
	Positive impact	• I recognise challenges. • I can usually foresee potential problems. • I deal with issues promptly. • I set realistic expectations.	• I cope well with contingencies. • Others believe I take matters seriously. • I tend to spot problems before they happen.

Reflect on your empathy

Here is a list of typical thoughts, feelings and actions associated with empathy.

1. Please circle all phrases in each row that apply to the way you work.

2. Each time you circle a 'Negative impact' characteristic, please colour a circle on your 'Priority topics for emotional resilience' worksheet.

Very high	Negative impact	• I have difficulty with people-related decisions. • I allow others' feelings to cloud my judgement. • I have too much empathy at the expense of meeting goals. • I find it hard to communicate expectations or enforce performance standards.	• I let people get away with their mistakes and do not hold them accountable. • Others' needs come before my own. • I discount my own intuitions about people and situations in preference for facts.
	Positive impact	• I am able to put myself in others' shoes. • I listen attentively to others. • I appreciate different viewpoints. • I build good rapport with others.	• I am good at developing other people's strengths. • I am good at understanding other people's goals and concerns. • I am a good mentor or coach for others.
Medium/balanced	Typical behaviours	• I listen and understand people's viewpoints. • I make an effort to understand. • I focus on both task and people. • I keep focused on my goals.	• I communicate openly. • I take a balanced approach on empathy – not too much, not too little. • I take each person on their own merits.
Very low	Negative impact	• I am unable to understand other people's feelings. • I do not value others' views. • I have difficulty in reading interpersonal cues. • I am perceived as uncaring.	• I am unlikely to adapt to specific people and situations. • I am insensitive. • My low empathy affects the quality of relationships I have.
	Positive impact	• I am logical/factual. • I stay on-track with important tasks. • I have clarity of focus. • I have firm judgement.	• I am comfortable enforcing standards. • I hold people responsible for their mistakes. • I do not tolerate excuses.

Reflect on your understanding

Here is a list of typical thoughts, feelings and actions associated with understanding.

1. Please circle all phrases in each row that apply to the way you work.

2. Each time you circle a 'Negative impact' characteristic, please colour a circle on your 'Priority topics for emotional resilience' worksheet.

Very high	Negative impact	• I am overly preoccupied with thinking about others. • I focus excessively on other people's needs. • I am easily distracted. • People perceive me as a negative influence on other people.	• My interest in others can be invasive. • I over-react to perceived threats. • I get unnecessarily anxious about other people's needs being met.
	Positive impact	• I am highly perceptive – emotionally and socially. • I am personable. • I value others. • I am sensitive to other people.	• I am good at reading others' concerns and needs. • I have a good understanding of other people. • I handle conflict effectively.
Medium/ balanced	Typical behaviours	• I understand both my own and other people's feelings. • I find common ground with colleagues. • I make an effort to help solve colleagues' problems.	• I maintain a balanced detachment. • I am not intrusive. • I respect other people's needs for personal space. • I keep problems in perspective.
Very low	Negative impact	• I am unable to name others' feelings. • I misinterpret other people's feelings. • I do not listen attentively. • I have difficulty in predicting other people's behaviour.	• I am not in tune with others' strengths and weaknesses. • I misread social and interpersonal cues. • I am self-absorbed and insensitive.
	Positive impact	• I am unemotional. • I concentrate well. • I make tough decisions that negatively affect others.	• I am thick-skinned and take criticism well. • I recover quickly from setbacks. • I am level headed and emotionally robust. • I keep calm under stress.

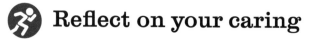

Reflect on your caring

Here is a list of typical thoughts, feelings and actions associated with caring.

1. Please circle all phrases in each row that apply to the way you work.

2. Each time you circle a 'Negative impact' characteristic, please colour a circle on your 'Priority topics for emotional resilience' worksheet.

High Negative impact	• I care overly for others at the sacrifice of getting my own work done. • I want to be involved in other people's business. • I neglect my needs over other people's needs. • I am overly self-conscious.	• I view ability to care for other people as a strength. • I judge people on the basis of how much they care. • I often feel resentful about how much I care.
High Positive impact	• I am kind, thoughtful and sympathetic about other people's stresses. • I gain the confidence and support of bosses, wider team, stakeholders. • I am unlikely to be cynical, moody or hostile.	• I present bad news in a caring way. • I am patient with others' mistakes. • I am unlikely to take criticism personally. • I give honest feedback.
Balanced Typical behaviours	• I am good at regulating my emotions when other people speak. • I connect well with people in upsetting situations. • I have a healthy tone in all communications.	• I give compliments publicly for other people's good work. • I feel comfortable socially. • I say thank you often. • I appreciate the role that other people play as part of success.
Low Negative impact	• I have no time for other people's needs. • I am uncomfortable discussing sensitive issues. • I do not seek spontaneous emotional responses from others. • I struggle to put people at ease.	• I am impatient with other people. • I find it difficult to build rapport with other people. • I prefer to work alone/am naturally reserved.
Low Positive impact	• I take a cautious approach with others. • I am more technically minded than people-minded. • I am task-focused and not easily distracted. • I deliver on promises made.	• I am comfortable working autonomously. • I am not swayed by other people's personal needs. • I am able to make unpopular decisions.

Start point: self reflection

Instructions *(continued)*

When you have circled all the characteristics that apply to you, and have calculated the total number of 'Negative impact' statements using the worksheet, do the following:

1. Notice where you have the greatest number of 'Negative impact' scores and start to read about your priority topics in Part 1: Essentials.

2. At the end of each chapter in Part 1, you will find an emotional resilience map, which signposts you to specific Skills and Results areas, to help focus your reading of Part 2: Skills and Part 3: Results. This will help you to navigate around the book.

3. I recommend you work through the Essential where you had the highest number of 'Negative impact' characteristics circled (including the related skills and results from the emotional resilience map at the end of the chapter). Then return to the Essential where you had the next highest number of 'Negative impact' characteristics and, again, work through the related Skills and Results.

4. Continue to do this until you have worked through all your Essentials with highest numbers of 'Negative impacts'.

5. If, after doing this, you wish to have a more comprehensive assessment of your emotional resilience, you can access an app and a survey tool from **eiworld.org/emotionalresilience**. You can also do a 360-degree assessment of your emotional resilience by having other people rate you and comment on your emotional resilience from their observation of you at work.

DEVELOPING EMOTIONAL RESILIENCE

	Essentials	Skills	Results
PERSONAL RESILIENCE Handling your emotions	**Self-worth** Feelings about yourself and how you function at work. **Self-control** Keeping your feelings under control in response to everyday work events. **Mood** Your emotional state in any given moment.	**Shifting** Changing your emotional state in response to everyday events. **Problem solving** Resolving problems of a personal, emotional or interpersonal nature by tuning into emotions as data.	**Energy** Sustaining your strength and vitality to perform at your best. **Thriving** Organising yourself to be effective under pressure.
TEAM RESILIENCE Handling emotions in interactions with others	**Empathy** Tuning into other people's feelings so that you can take them on board when making decisions. **Understanding** Tuning into what colleagues need in order for them to be effective at work. **Caring** Showing that other people matter so that colleagues are able to make their best effort at work.	**Expressing** Communicating your feelings and thoughts to others at work. **Group empathy** Tuning into and shifting emotions at group level to stay on track with your work goals. **Dialogue** Discussing feelings when there is a problem.	**Connection** Building relationships through personal interactions. **Influence** Leading and managing relationships with stakeholders, colleagues and team members.

© Ei World Limited

Part 1

The Essentials

The **Essentials** consist of handling your own and others' feelings. You are invited to use your self-understanding to prioritise the **skills** to focus on, to build **results** in personal and team resilience.

Personal resilience

There are three vital building blocks for understanding the core of your personal resilience.

Acting as a barometer of how you feel about yourself, your **self-worth** is reflected in your inner dialogue and your outward confidence. **Self-control** determines how you respond to everyday work scenarios. Problems in controlling yourself can lead to misunderstandings and conflict.

Your **mood** is the volume of positive energy you bring to interactions reflecting your attitudes towards the past, present and future.

PERSONAL RESILIENCE

SELF-WORTH   SELF-CONTROL   MOOD

Team resilience

There are three vital building blocks for understanding the core of your team resilience.

Our personal success at work does not take place in a vacuum, our workplaces are increasingly complex and rely on working with and through colleagues who we count on for knowledge, information and ideas.

We know that emotion is present in every communication we have with people in our team. Events in a team can trigger a variety of emotional states. When you are feeling a sense of threat or that you are out on a limb, you will withdraw your contribution in interactions with others. When you are feeling supported by the team, you are likely to inject a productive interaction with your colleagues. Emotion brings with it both threats and opportunities.

It is clear that our workplace is a human ecosystem where our actions and reactions to each other cause impact and effects both within the team and beyond. Our success at work depends on the quality of our relationships with colleagues, customers and key stakeholders. This is the subject of the following three chapters: **empathy**, **understanding** and **caring** as a counter-balance to selfishness or trying to be successful on our own.

The question is how to cultivate these Essentials, so that we can get the best results with and through others. These three chapters provide you with a quality assurance system for the interactions that are important to your work success.

By focusing on six **Essentials** in Part 1, you will play your part to create the type of workplace that we all desire, where you and your work colleagues feel understood, connected, valued and able to give your best to each other and to the organisation.

A core principle of ancient Buddhist philosophy is that there is interconnection and interdependence between all living and inanimate things. In the last three decades, developments in physics have given us clear evidence of this.

There are connections between the six **Essentials** and I invite you on a journey to look into these in more detail as you work through the book.

Chapter 1

Self-worth

'A person's worth in this world is estimated according to the value they put on themselves.'

JEAN DE LA BRUYERE, FRENCH PHILOSOPHER AND MORALIST

This chapter will help you understand:

- how self-worth is a core aspect of both *what* you do and *how* you do it;
- how self-worth stems from early life messages and how secure you feel in your relationships with other people;
- the true value that you bring to your work – your identity, purpose and uniqueness;
- steps for working on your self-worth, including how to deal with your negative self-talk, healthy behaviours and how to set yourself up for success, whatever the situation.

Self-worth
Feelings about yourself and how you function at work

Self-worth is a combination of self-respect and personal belief that you make a unique contribution at work. This is not easy in practice as your self-worth is built from a very early age. Self-worth is not just an inner aspect of ourself, it affects how others experience you, how you do your work and, ultimately, your reputation.

Healthy self-worth enables you to connect well with others and to have good relationships without stress or conflict. Many people in the workplace do not seem to have healthy self-worth.

Self-worth is the overall result of the everyday commentary in our heads about ourselves. It is a powerful starting point, as the way in which we perceive ourselves through our inner talk becomes our reality. What we tell ourselves about ourselves creates who we are.

Our self-worth is driven by our inner voice that tells us whether or not we are good enough in relation to how we view other people. For most people, early life experiences determine how much we value ourselves and, in turn, how others value us. To counter this, we must choose our thoughts, behaviours and reactions carefully so that we can make healthy choices.

Practical observations

1. In my experience, many senior leaders are insecure overachievers. This is revealed often in reactions to compliments I give about their professional achievements. Even the most impressive leaders look very embarrassed and nearly always mutter something like, 'You are just being nice to me.' We will have evolved in business when leaders can learn to accept compliments with a simple 'thank you'.

2. Many people in work associate their self-worth with their job level/ salary and often make unfavourable comparisons to others who they perceive as being more successful (external aspects), rather than with the positive qualities of how they do their job or how they feel about their job (internal aspects). To work on self-worth requires us to be able to notice both the signs of our success as well as to change how we feel about how we do our work.

3. Our level of self-worth is a significant factor in how we build relationships with others. It also affects our health (see next section 'What you need to know') and our work in teams. Two people with reasonable self-worth usually establish a clear communication. Two people, both with lower self-worth or with mixed self-worth (one higher and one lower) often will interpret what the other person says through their own low self-image. Unexpected tensions and disagreements can surface. Therefore, it is one **essential** on which to spend time and you will notice that this is the longest chapter in this book. It is core to your emotional resilience.

⚙ WHAT YOU NEED TO KNOW

1. It was thought previously that self-esteem was most important for adolescents. Recent research has studied self-worth in adults and has given us evidence that self-worth affects us biologically. Research shows that feelings of low self-worth are associated with higher levels of the stress hormone, cortisol. Feelings of high self-worth are associated with lower levels of cortisol. People with a history of stress or depression have the strongest association between the stress hormone cortisol and self-worth (and how much cortisol goes up or down in relation to self-worth). It is important to pay attention to this aspect of emotional resilience because cortisol is also linked with a variety of illnesses. Interestingly, as self-esteem increases, we produce less cortisol. If it reduces, we produce more cortisol. This is a good reason to work on your self-worth; maintaining or improving your self-worth helps prevent health problems (Liu, Wrosch, Miller and Pruessner, 2014).

2. Self-worth is important throughout our lives. It tends to increase during adolescence, and then decrease in young adulthood. Self-worth rises steadily as we age, but starts declining around the time of retirement. In adults, there is no significant difference between the self-worth of men and women during either of those life phases, even though it is often assumed that men have higher self-worth.

3. Self-worth depends on the ratio between expectation and success. People develop low self-worth either because their expectations are too high or because they achieve too few successes (William James, 1890 quoted in Csikzsentmihalyi, 1997). It can be useful to consider how our expectations affect our self-worth.

MEET ANTHONY

Anthony spent many years at an international company. However, his low self-worth meant he was overlooked frequently for promotion. He felt he was never good enough and unconsciously conveyed this feeling in his interactions with others at work. His self-confidence was low, as he believed not having English as his first language was too big a disadvantage. He had no ambitions to change job and would have spent the rest of his life there doing the same thing! He lived in shared rented accommodation and found it stressful living with someone he did not know well and with whom he did not have much in common.

Unfortunately, the company was subject to a buyout and it was clear that Anthony was about to lose his job. Fortunately, he was able to work with a coach who helped him to examine why he was so negative about himself. He was comparing himself unfavourably to others' skills and abilities. This clearly had to be replaced by more positive feelings. He learnt some mindfulness techniques to help him avoid getting side-tracked into negativity. He worked at becoming more focused and determined in his career and started to see his talents, which he had failed to appreciate, more positively. His new-found self-confidence resulted in him taking a high-level job, and he now lives in South America.

Observe people at work who you have a gut instinct have healthy self-worth:

- Who do you know at work who looks and sounds confident in most situations? Note at least two names of people who match this description.

- How do they sound? What words do you hear them using that explicitly or implicitly express confidence?

- What do you notice about their physical appearance? What do they wear? What do they do to look after themselves?

- If you could guess, what do you think they say to themselves (internal dialogue) on a typical day?

- Which aspects of how they carry themselves and behave would you like to demonstrate more of yourself?

Use these questions to observe yourself:

- When you think about your strengths and weaknesses together, what words could you use to describe yourself?

- For what attributes, skills or qualities do others seek you out?

- When you judge yourself, is it in a punitive, self-dismissive kind of way? Or do you leave room to forgive yourself, move on and create the possibility to improve and change?

- What do you notice about other people's opinions of you? Do you notice and acknowledge the positives as well as the negatives? Do you react to each in the same way? (E.g. do you dismiss the positives and focus only on the negatives?)

Early life messages

The challenge in this essential is that our level of self-worth is deep-rooted and many psychologists would suggest that you require therapy to create a shift. Babies are born with a decent amount of self-worth. But, as we develop, the experiences, attitudes and comments received from significant others can erode this. How we were treated in our early years usually affects how we feel about ourselves. As children, our self-worth depended on whether or not our basic needs were met (later you will be invited to rate your early life experiences against seven basic needs).

Often, our unmet basic needs produce in us everyday challenges until we can learn to fulfil our own needs. As adults in the workplace, some of us are operating still from old drummed-in messages. We are perfectionists and relentless in getting things right, so we do not give ourselves a break. We feel we need to be charitable and to take care of others before our own needs. We put other people first out of fear of being perceived as selfish and then we do not achieve what we desire for ourselves. We hide our light so that others will not feel uncomfortable with our successes. We feel anxious and blame ourselves when things go wrong.

It can be helpful to distinguish between being passionate about your work and medicating on your work. Passion means that you are gaining from it and doing it because you love it. Medicating is when your passion becomes a problem because it affects your balance; people complain you are not available and you have problems in relationships. Work can become your 'higher power' when you do not have secure relationships and attachments.

The first step is to ask ourselves if our basic needs have been met.

Reflections to improve self-worth

 ## 1. Basic needs

Seven basic needs are listed below based on the work of Dr Ted Klontz. This activity forces you to notice how challenging it may be to develop a healthy sense of self-worth. If one or more of these are unmet, then it is likely that you will have to work harder at building your self-worth. If we have grown up with all these needs met, we will bring a healthy level of self-worth to the workplace.

Consider your early childhood and try to score each one of these basic needs on a scale of fully unmet to fully met:

Need	Problem behaviours in early life when this need was unmet	Scoring instructions
Right to be Approximate age: Pre-utero and birth	Child feels the stress from distressed parents, the living environment, other traumas or stresses.	Review the seven needs and problem behaviours and decide how many of these needs were:
Right to have needs Approximate age: Birth to 18 months	Clingy. Look to external world to get own needs met. Parents' needs come first before child. Child ends up meeting parents' needs whilst own needs not met. Co-dependency (see Chapter 4 Empathy), particularly if parents are alcoholics (or substance addicted) and child ends up feeling like they have to take care of the parents.	**Fully unmet** in your childhood? No. of needs: ___ **Somewhat unmet** in your childhood? No. of needs: ___
Right to separate Approximate age: Pre-school years and toddlers	Parents have anxiety about the child being apart and pull the child in. Leads to mistrust, independence without being supported, and throws off life development. Does not feel complete without a mate.	**Unsure/hard** to know? No. of needs: ___
Right to speak my truth Approximate age: Middle school	Lack of expression ends up in addictive behaviour or saying hurtful things to people you love and not having people to share your truth with. Do not ask for help. Cannot say no. Voice does not matter to others.	**Somewhat met** in your childhood? No. of needs: ___ **Fully met** in your childhood? No. of needs: ___
Right to autonomy with support Approximate age: 12–18	Difficulty making decisions. Sitting on the fence. Not doing what you want to do in life and work.	
Right to love and passion Approximate age: 18–45	Relationship problems.	
Right to your own spiritual path Approximate age: Any	Rebellion. Difficult to tolerate others' opinions, if own were not respected.	

Our unmet needs affect not only what we do but how we do it. This is most apparent usually in periods of adversity or challenge at work. It includes beliefs about oneself (for example, I am competent/incompetent, I am liked/disliked) and associated emotions about oneself (for example, I feel triumph, despair, pride or shame). It is also reflected in behaviours, such as having dialogue with people at work or our ease in expressing emotions.

To think more about how the unmet needs affected us, it can be useful to look at our work lives to date, in terms of highs and lows.

2. Attachment

This reflection activity enables you to decide how much of a problem your level of self-worth is. Review each of the columns below and decide which column best describes you.

Insecure attachment	Secure attachment	Avoidant attachment
I feel less than you. I am not ok, you are ok. I cannot meet my own needs. I look to others to meet my needs. Fear of abandonment.	I feel equal. I am ok, you are ok. Born with rights intact. Have good healthy physical, emotional, social boundaries. Comfortable with self.	I feel better than you. I'm ok, you are not ok. Unaware and disowning of personal needs. Hyper-controlling. Detached.
Fundamental problem is that you did not get what you needed at the time.	No fundamental problem as you had a healthy mum and a healthy dad.	Fundamental problem is that you got too much of something.

Source: based on Ainsworth and Bowlby (1991) on attachment styles

Activities to improve self-worth

 1. Reducing critical self-talk

A tip for building more self-respect is to notice and remove your negative language in your everyday work. Do you complain endlessly to yourself about your work, your boss and your colleagues either openly in your conversations with colleagues and friends, or under your breath?

When you have a frustrating day or when you are not achieving what you want, make a chart and on one side list all the times you said to yourself, 'I should do X.' Then try to change the 'should' to 'want' and see how you feel about the statement. Do this for each statement. Review the list and keep only the ones that you really want, or at least change the balance (for example, for the next day) so that there are more wants than shoulds.

2. Healthy me

Not feeling good about yourself can affect virtually all aspects of the way you do your work, how you dress, how you speak, how you interact with others. There are typical counterproductive behaviours that accompany low self-worth.

List all the things you can do each week to look after yourself, including:

- nutrition (enough water, regular meals, healthy eating);
- exercise (individual exercise you enjoy as well as team sports);
- friends and contacts at work (who nurtures you and how can you spend more time with them?);
- define what you want to create in your workplace and take action to make it happen;
- identify the rocks of your work life and do not compromise them for anyone or anything (rocks are the most important things to you – your

specific special relationships, fun projects you like, your self-care needs on a daily basis, etc.)

- identify who you can talk to about emotional or personal challenges.

3. Healthy interactions

As you have now looked at your everyday activities, we can move onto some suggestions for handling the everyday interactions with other people. This is an important focus. Be ready for others reacting negatively to a more confident you. This is natural. You will gain more respect as you develop your self-worth.

Use the ideas below to build healthy interactions. There are seven here; try to apply one per day for a week.

1. Build resources of work friendships around you to support you.

2. Keep a note of when someone says something positive and affirming about you at work.

3. Learn to listen, trust and express your own feelings and do not automatically respond to the feelings of others. When demands are placed on you, respond with what works for you rather than what works better for everyone except you – see Chapter 9 Expressing.

4. Respect your time and value what you are giving out to others. Do not give more time to things than you have decided is balanced.

 You can access a web resource on setting healthy boundaries and creating healthy balance between competing areas of work life and life in general.

5. Seek out and spend more time with people who affirm your skills, self-worth and contribution. Seek out positive mentors who can share their experiences and offer guidance on your career.

6. Stop people-pleasing at self-cost. Use the energy to focus on your own desires so that you can make the choices that are right for you.

7. Support yourself by asking for help when you need it.

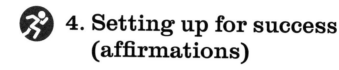

4. Setting up for success (affirmations)

This is one of the most powerful exercises for working on your self-worth. If you have not encountered affirmations before, it can sound unusual work to do. The hard work is writing them. Once you have written them down, you can use them daily. Many clients have benefited from this, including Anthony, whose story you heard earlier.

1. Write a personalised list of your key strengths and qualities. Aim to write a minimum of 50 statements in short sentences. This can sound really hard at first. You could choose to draft 10 at a time. Write sentences with these stems:

   - I can...
   - I am able to...
   - I am good at....
   - I am proud of...
   - I am...

   All statements need to be positive without being self-effacing. Include activities that you are good at, citing personal skills that you have.

2. If you get stuck, use the list at the end of this exercise for inspiration to compile your own. This was from a client called Julia, who we will meet later (in Chapter 15 Influence).

    An electronic version of this exercise is available in the web resources so that you can adapt the lists easily.

3. When you have your list, keep it handy on your phone or tablet for when you have a spare moment (for example, standing in a queue or travelling on a train).

Use this list to choose the qualities that will help you in a specific interaction (for example, when you are about to go into a meeting with other colleagues or clients). Ahead of a specific interaction, pick out three affirmations that will help increase your confidence. What evidence could you use? For example, ahead of a meeting with your boss, choose the affirmations of:

- 'I have good technical knowledge.'
- 'I am good at explaining complex aspects of the problem.'
- 'I am good at building rapport in a tense situation.'

Your evidence for these are:

- 'I interject my technical knowledge into the dialogue.'
- 'I draw some simple diagrams to explain the complex process we are designing.'
- 'I am able to describe a few facts at the end of the meeting about how my boss' thinking changed through the skills I showed in the meeting.'

Example affirmations

1. I listen well.

2. I am considerate.

3. I am an effective team member.

4. I can form healthy relationships with other people.

5. I am very self-disciplined.

6. I am emotionally strong.

7. I am intellectually able.

8. I present well.

9. I communicate effectively both verbally and in writing.

10. I am a role model.

 You can download a full list of over 70 affirmations from the web resources.

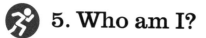

5. Who am I?

This activity helps you to state your core talents. This is highly useful for influencing your work progression and finding focus in what you are doing.

You will be stating your identity, gift and purpose very succinctly. This can have many uses – it is a form of elevator speech if someone asks you to tell them about yourself. Rather than mumble some basic facts, it helps you get straight to what you are good at. When I coach people, I use this activity to help people cut through the large volume of words we use and get straight to the essence of what they do well at work. Once you have written this for yourself and you are happy with it, you might want to make a poster of it and hang it on your wall.

Identity – who you are in three words; choose three qualities that describe how you do your work.

Uniqueness – in one to three words, write a statement of your unique talent.

Purpose – in one sentence take a broad view of the meaning of your work and what you are here to do.

Use this as a sort of mission statement every day so that you can allow yourself to be in charge of your own work life. Here are some examples:

Geetu: Who I am is someone who is authentic, pioneering and challenging; my gift is insight; my purpose is to help people evolve.

Anabelle (a project manager): Who I am is someone who is caring, organised and intelligent. My gift is building processes that work; my purpose is to make the organisation function effectively.

You may wish to validate your self-perceptions by seeking out feedback from others.

 You can download a template for a poster from the web resources so you can display this close to your place of work.

Quick tips for reducing high self-worth

Some people have the reverse problem, of high self-worth, so they need to reduce the outward signs of it. This section shows how to keep your self-worth in check if your self-worth is higher than is ideal for the work context you are in right now.

Many of our workplaces emphasise competition, individuality and personal gain over others. So these tips might be helpful in some work contexts for building more effective relationships with others and developing respect from others. They will be useful if you have a big ego in the way of your success!

Do more of the following:

Self

1. Decide on who you are going to help as a way to be humble about what you have and to increase the number of people you support.

2. Let go of your preconceived ideas and take on the belief that you do not know as much as you think you do.

3. Do not judge other people. Whenever you do, try to judge yourself instead.

4. Note the time you spend talking versus listening and aim to shift the balance so that others express themselves to you more than you do to them. Remember that listening is not the space before you talk!

5. Remember all the things you are not good at doing.

6. Remember that everyone, including you, makes mistakes.

7. Remember that you are not perfect. Recognise your weaknesses.

8. Remember that you are not the best at anything and there is always room for improvement.

9. Remember that your goal is to be better than how you used to be,

and this might require some humility to work on the areas that are less strong in your everyday functioning at work.

10. Remind yourself that you are not an island; you need others to be successful too.

11. Spend more time in nature as a way to balance yourself and realise how small and simple you are in the world compared to the power, complexity, size and depth of nature.

12. Set yourself a one-minute limit every time you talk about yourself or something good you have done – and stick to it.

To work further on self-worth, I recommend you consider going next to the skills and results areas highlighted below:

EMOTIONAL RESILIENCE MAP SELF-WORTH

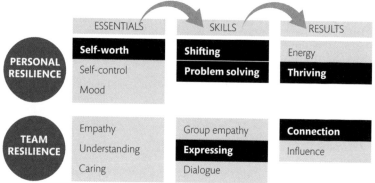

	ESSENTIALS	SKILLS	RESULTS
PERSONAL RESILIENCE	**Self-worth** Self-control Mood	**Shifting** **Problem solving**	Energy **Thriving**
TEAM RESILIENCE	Empathy Understanding Caring	Group empathy **Expressing** Dialogue	**Connection** Influence

Chapter 2

Self-control

'Only in quiet waters do things mirror themselves undistorted.

Only in a quiet mind is adequate perception of the world.'

HANS MARGOLIUS, AMERICAN AUTHOR

This chapter will give you:

- an understanding of how your self-control is vital for being effective at work and progressing your career;

- a perspective on the unlimited number of emotion triggers, distractions and activity in a typical work day;

- steps for working on your self-control, including how to deal with your anger and how to analyse emotions that arise;

- a list of actions you can display at work to increase your self-control.

Self-control
Keeping your feelings under control in response to everyday work events

Self-control is being still and controlled on the inside so that we demonstrate calm and measured action on the outside, or restraint on our instinctive responses. It is about how we deal with distractions, impulses, feelings and reactions. It is essential to develop, as our self-control acutely affects how we respond to everyday events at work.

The steady stream of triggers that can cause reactions at work is endless: emails, calls, texts, social media chat, meetings, requests for urgent responses, unexpected work schedule changes, travel disruption, exploding scandals that force us into crisis management mode or Acts of God that throw our country into a state of emergency.

There are also the time-stealing gremlins when technology fails, phones, computers and tablets crash, or a sudden power cut grinds our work to a halt. Our self-control is constantly being tested at work!

Self-control is also the extent to which we can take control of our dysfunctional (unhealthy) behaviour. This does not mean that healthy spontaneity or impulsiveness have to be avoided. At work, those with effective self-control usually think before acting, reflecting carefully before making decisions. Although they weigh all the information before they make up their mind, they are not overly cautious.

Those with very low self-control tend to be impetuous and give in to their urges. In such states, much like children, we want immediate gratification. We speak without having thought things through and change our minds frequently. I remember in my first job in a well-known bank, noticing that one of my peers could not resist the temptation to smoke a cigar. So, even though the situation was a very formal dinner with the bank's executives, she reached for a cigar. This was regarded as immature, inappropriate behaviour by senior executives and was damaging to her reputation early in her career.

Practical observations

1. My observation is that many people have self-control issues at work. The first sign of this is almost always apparent in someone's appearance. Are they in shape? Do they seem like they are in control of themselves and their patterns?

2. Another telling sign of self-control is how a typical meeting takes place at your workplace. Do people tend to jump in and want to hear their own voices? Or is it very calm, organised and effective? Do meetings start and end on time?

3. A further observation is that distractions are increasing and, with this, our self-control problems (see the key theme in this chapter).

 WHAT YOU NEED TO KNOW

1. Researchers have found very strong links between self-control and career success. People with greater self-control perform better at work. A now famous experiment by Walter Mischel and colleagues at Stanford University, 'The Marshmallow Test,' assessed the self-control of four-year-old children. Each child was given a marshmallow and asked not to eat it for 20 minutes. The reward for resisting would be a second marshmallow. The teacher left the classroom.

Some children ate the marshmallow before the teacher even left the room! Others were able to resist for a few minutes; and some for the entire 20 minutes.

Over 20 years, the researchers followed these children to capture their outcomes in life. They found a direct link between delayed gratification and academic performance, earnings, mental health, well-being and happiness up to 20 years later in life. The children who were able to meet the challenge by controlling their desire, had better positive outcomes in life, both academically and professionally.

Mischel has recently published a book describing more recent findings that the best way to work on self-control is to find a substitute image for the one you are trying to resist (Mischel, 2014).

2. In a follow-up study at Duke University, researchers followed 1,000 children for 30 years. They studied the effect of early self-control on health, wealth and public safety. Their research showed that individuals with lower self-control experienced negative outcomes in all three areas, for example, more sexually transmitted diseases, substance abuse, financial problems (including poor credit and lack of savings), lone parenting and crime.

3. When we are hungry, or tired, we are more likely to struggle with self-control and more likely to display aggression, irrational decision making, as well as sexual or financial impulsiveness. Supermarkets usually place chocolate by the till for this reason. We are more likely to give in to the temptation when we are tired.

MEET IMRAN

Imran took over the management of a large organisation with prestigious clients but soon found himself out of his depth. Being reasonably new to the role, he did not feel confident in declining to take on extra duties when asked. Rather than assessing the level of work he was already committed to and making a clear decision on whether he had the capacity for anything further, he would just say 'Yes' to seem obliging and 'for the good of the organisation'. He also had constant interruptions from phone calls, email enquiries and other members of staff with problems.

He was soon working all hours and worrying about meeting deadlines. His relationships and personal health were suffering and he was also receiving complaints from his boss and clients if everything was not 100 per cent. Previously very fit, Imran found little time for exercise and his energy was depleted. His sleep pattern was also poor.

Coaching helped Imran to see that he needed to take control and better structure his working life. He needed to take the time to consider what duties he could feasibly take on, rather than jumping straight in and agreeing to everything everyone wanted of him; set aside a specific time of day to respond to emails or calls; and not think everything must be done immediately.

He also acknowledged that he harboured unexpressed anger about the way he felt he was being treated. He arranged to have a meeting with his boss where they discussed openly one another's expectations and came to an agreement about a more flexible working arrangement and more support for Imran.

 Observe people at work who you consider to have healthy self-control:

- Who achieves successful outcomes, resisting their urges to act or speak, even when they have strong feelings about something?
- What is the maximum number of times this person might interrupt someone in a natural conversation or be impatient or finish the other person's sentences? (Ask them if you are not sure.)
- What is the maximum number of times this person might raise their voice in a discussion to get their point heard?

- Which aspects of the observed behaviour would you like to incorporate into your behaviour more often?

Use these questions to observe yourself:

- What are my body language signs of low self-control?

  For example, breaking eye contact, tapping fingers or feet, waiting to interrupt, interrupting and breaking in.

- What sensations do I feel when I exercise low or high self-control?

  For example, low self-control: tightness in chest or shoulders, holding breath, gnawing in pit of stomach, rushing feeling in the mind.

Dealing with distractions

A major issue at work is distraction and the sheer volume of inputs that we have coming in.

Imagine that you are at your desk, working in a relaxed state and getting a lot done. Your mobile phone rings and it is a blocked number. What do you do?

- Do you answer it, ignore it or send it to voicemail?

- If you answer it, why do you do that?

- Is it because you want to know who is calling? Is it because it is your habit and what you would do naturally?

- Is it because you have learned to be available to people?

The phone has taken you away from your work and is a good example of how self-control affects us constantly. The key point here is that you have a choice: you can leave the phone ringing and ignore it, and continue with your original plan.

With our increasing reliance on technology and online promotions constantly vying for our attention, we are being encouraged endlessly to do things **now** rather than later. In the face of these urges, our reaction defines how well we can stay on track with our tasks and our goals.

Self-control is about remembering we have a choice. How we respond to events normally distinguishes the outstanding from the mediocre professional. Our level of self-control can be the difference between failure and success. Responding to a new opportunity in time while there is still an opening, can help us to get a job. Taking a reasonable amount of time to overcome initial anxiety about an urgent request before responding to your boss, can be extremely helpful. But how do we know whether it is appropriate to respond slowly or quickly? And what is our natural default in terms of speed of reaction?

I find that very physical actions can help us to build the self-control we need – having a drink of water opens up the brain centre that deals with control; doing square breathing (in for four, hold for four, out for four, and hold for four) can be very beneficial. These experiential changes in our bodies change our brain chemistry. When in doubt, drink water and breathe. This is a tip I offer executives who have problems with self-control in meetings.

Working on your self-control

Lower self-control is often the result of challenges in one or more of the other areas of emotional resilience. Using the exercises in the self-worth and mood sections will support your efforts to work on your self-control.

Those without self-control are more likely to make mistakes at work that have dire consequences. Hastily made decisions we regret later, inappropriate remarks at meetings, lack of kindness and respect for others, not listening: these are all behaviours that undermine being a successful professional.

Self-control affects not only what we do but how we do it. As adults in the workplace, some of us operate with very low self-control – always needing to be first in the queue, interrupting people in meetings, swearing inappropriately with colleagues or our bosses. We do not censor ourselves and operate in a fast, primal way. Usually this is most apparent in times of high stress at work.

Our self-control allows us to take a careful approach to our work, our self-presentation and our relationships. Like self-worth, our self-control is a key aspect of how we are at work. When someone asks us a question, do we jump in and reply right away or do we naturally use words like, 'Let me think about that' or 'Let me get back to you on that'?

Healthy self-control at work involves getting into the habit of constantly being aware of how we are engaging with others; not instantly revealing our first reactions without proper reflection; not making assumptions or judging situations without first understanding that there may be different perspectives. Building up better self-control leads to stronger emotional resilience at work; people are less likely to be blown away in the first wind. They remain calm, restrained and composed in the face of pressure, dealing well with unexpected challenges and failures. They learn from experience and make good decisions. Controlling our impulses is key to self-control. These are learnable skills. It involves recognising that we have a choice and that we can decide what is appropriate moment to moment.

Not having sufficient control over ourselves affects every aspect of the way we work: how we speak, interact, work through our tasks. There are typical counterproductive behaviours that accompany low self-control. We are impatient, we want everything done our way, we do not want to listen to what others might have to say. As with self-worth, often we can engage in unhealthy habits around eating, smoking or drinking alcohol to numb ourselves against feelings we may have about ourselves. Those with low self-control often have problems with diet, exercise, work habits, addictions and emotional behaviour. This is reflected in a low level of awareness, affecting our ability to operate at our full potential at work.

Reflections to improve self-control

If, routinely, we respond to everything rapidly, with little thought and a determined sense of urgency, there may be some benefits. We might get many tasks done in a small amount of time, no matter how tough the tasks. But the consequences can include omissions, mistakes or inappropriate behaviour towards others.

The reality is that, whatever we do, we can never escape from dealing with some emotional content at work, and we need to be able to exercise some control over our responses. Self-control is not just about how we react to one event and experience the immediate consequences or fallout. It also more widely affects how others experience us, how we do our work and, ultimately, our reputation.

Our self-control is driven by an inner voice that tells us whether or not we have to move at speed. Early life traumas determine how much we are able to control ourselves and, in turn, how much we are able to act responsibly in the face of choices available to us.

There are two essential reflections. Together, these will give you a full sense of how effective your self-control is at work:

- **Mismanaged anger** – as anger can be a key source of self-control issues, this exercise encourages you to be proactive about what you feel angry about, so that your self-control challenges do not get the better of you.

- **Event behaviour consequence (EBC) analysis** – this activity is designed to give you some practice in understanding where emotions come from and the decisions that we can make as a result.

1. Mismanaged anger

'The cyclone derives its powers from a calm center. So does a person.'

NORMAN VINCENT PEALE, AMERICAN MINISTER AND AUTHOR

Mismanaged anger, or unexpressed anger, can not only get in the way of healthy relationships but can also damage them forever. This activity encourages you to identify your 'hot buttons' – things that your colleagues do that annoy you or make you lose your temper. In this activity it is recommended that you identify the frequency of these hot buttons and the action you choose in response. There are three steps involved:

Step 1. List the situations that annoy you, frustrate you or anger you about your colleagues.

Step 2. Now rank these by adding a number next to each one to identify the frequency with which these occur – ranging from 1 (most frequent) to 10 (least frequent).

Step 3. Now identify what you need to do about each one:

- forgive;
- forget about it;
- discuss it and express your view;
- acknowledge that you need to change this, otherwise the relationship or team will not function well;
- make a recommendation to the leader of the team.

Example

If you need inspiration to kick-start the process, here are some examples.

Situation	Rank	Action
Being told the same things about objectives and targets every day	7	Discuss
Experiencing the same issues and not solving them	4	Discuss
My manager not always doing what he/she says he/she is going to do	8	Forgive/discuss
Starting meetings late	5	Discuss
Always doing what one person in the team wants to do	3	Discuss
Absent manager leading me or others to pick up the pieces on problems or urgent situations	6	Forgive/discuss
Not having any free time together or time to socialise in the team	1	Acknowledge
An old hurt that is still hanging around from when a colleague let me down	9	Forget
Working late every night of the week	2	Acknowledge
Not enough time off or holidays taken in the team	10	Discuss

Now that you have identified the hot buttons in your everyday work life, take the time to address the ones that require a discussion. Provide equal time and space to air your view and the other person's view so that you can try to reach a middle ground. Many problems can be resolved just by identifying the areas of difficulty.

 # 2. Event behaviour consequence (EBC) analysis

This activity is designed to give you some practice in understanding where strong emotions come from and the decisions that we can make as a result.

We always have a choice in our responses between what is rational and what is irrational, and both of these paths have emotional and behavioural consequences. The psychologist Albert Ellis identified that every feeling has an activating event, which creates rational or irrational beliefs and self-talk, leading to consequences that are emotional and behavioural. This is called EBC analysis.

For example, take the feeling of being angry:

Event: anger might be triggered by an event, such as your manager or colleague criticising you.

Beliefs and self-talk: these are both rational and irrational. Examples of irrational beliefs and self-talk might be, 'How dare he? He never seems to be happy with what I do.' Rational beliefs and self-talk might include, 'He has a point. I haven't done my fair share of work in the team.'

Consequences: each belief and self-talk will have emotional or behavioural consequences. The irrational self-talk mentioned here ('How dare he?', etc.) may lead to anger or frustration, and the result (or behavioural consequence) is that I stop listening. The rational self-talk ('He has a point,' etc.) leads to only mild annoyance and results in greater listening.

Making decisions

Now complete an EBC analysis for five key emotions that are getting in your way. Select emotions that you would like to look at more closely and list, for each one, the **event**, the **beliefs and self-talk** (both rational and irrational) and the **consequences**. You may wish to focus on the emotions that you identified as obstacles to your effectiveness.

Feeling 1: _____

Event	Beliefs and Self-Talk	Consequences
	(irrational) →	
	(rational) →	

Feeling 2: _____

Event	Beliefs and Self-Talk	Consequences
	(irrational) →	
	(rational) →	

Feeling 3: _____

Event	Beliefs and Self-Talk	Consequences
	(irrational) →	
	(rational) →	

Feeling 4: _____

Event	Beliefs and Self-Talk	Consequences
	(irrational) →	
	(rational) →	

Feeling 5: _____

Event	Beliefs and Self-Talk	Consequences
	(irrational) →	
	(rational) →	

Now look back over this list and name the emotions that have the greatest consequences for how you work.

Activities to improve self-control

The best way to work on self-control is to actually practise it. It may sound obvious, but there is no other way. Here are three activities to help improve your self-control at work:

1. Step change

This is an exercise for taking immediate action on your self-control at work. It involves three simple activities:

1. Seek feedback from others on how effective you are being.

2. Avoid jumping to conclusions, and take time to reach decisions. Start using the language of, 'I can't answer that right now, but leave this with me and I will come back to you.'

3. Decide what is **core** and **non-core** to your work and where your energy is going to be best used.

2. Needs or urges?

Next time you feel low self-control coming on, for instance if you are about to make an impulsive decision, stop and go through the following process:

1. Ask yourself, what am I trying to satisfy here, a **need** or an **urge**?

2. Move from **urge** to **need** by postponing the decision, for instance to the next day.

3. The next day, test the **urge**. Has it changed? Does it have the same quality and/or intensity?

4. Now test the **need**. Has it changed? Does it have the same quality and/or intensity?

Ask yourself – what is more important to you: to satisfy needs or urges? Learning the difference between the two will help you build self-control.

When you have a frustrating day, or when you are not achieving what you want, list all the times you said to yourself, 'I should do X'. Then try to change the **should** to **want** and see how you feel about the statement. Do this for each statement.

Review the list and keep only the ones that you really want, or at least change the balance (for example, for the next day), so that **wants** appears more often than **shoulds**. This focus on needs is at the core of exercising self-control.

3. Action centre

These 15 actions are proven to help you to overcome self-control issues. Many of them are based on distracting your mind through your thoughts, actions and behaviours:

1. Act with a sense of self-responsibility in your everyday work. Set up a pattern of being in control. Have work objectives visible to you on a daily basis. Have a clear time plan and use a timer to keep you focused.

2. Do daily exercises/reflective work. Example: create a daily action plan; write notes on each meeting, observing people's behaviour; keep a reflective log of your thoughts and feelings about work.

3. Have scripts to allow you time to reflect on a situation. Example: 'I'd like some time to think about it.'

4. Have scripts to buy time to regain your composure. Example: 'I need to take five minutes to consider and I will be back after a quick break.'

5. Eat for mood management. The brain needs adequate protein to maintain proper blood sugar levels, which are related to mood and the ability to manage moods.

6. Physical exercise provides distraction but also helps balance the brain chemistry associated with emotion.

7. Energy management: plan activities based on your energy levels and be aware that these may change. (See the energy audit activity in Chapter 12 Energy.)

8. Learn to be an objective observer of your feelings. While you are observing, you will not be overwhelmed by your emotions. Being a better observer will help you identify more choices in how you can respond.

9. Make a list of situations and people that play a part in you losing control and try to analyse what really happens and why.

10. Practise 'the 20-minute solution': distract yourself for 20 minutes, the time the amygdala (storehouse of our emotion memories) needs to get back to equilibrium when we are flooded with emotion.

11. Self-discipline – do what you say and do not harm others (these are two laws that are agreed on in all religions).

12. Take control of your environment where you can. If you are constantly looking at your mobile phone, physically put it away or give it to someone else.

13. Avoid the thoughts/feelings and situations that challenge your ability to manage your impulses.

14. Try to avoid others who have low self-control problems.

15. When your energy levels are low, drink water. Do not miss regular meals. Watch out for excess or comfort eating when you are feeling hungry, lonely, angry or tired.

Quick tips for reducing self-control

Sometimes our self-control can be too high for the situation we are in. Typically, someone at work with very high self-control can be so restrained that they never react openly. Their control can be so high that you never really know what they are thinking. They can seem bored or overly detached as a cover-up for not feeling their emotions. They might be slow to react or not notice what is happening in the room. This can be almost as tricky as low self-control. Sometimes I hear people in meetings speak so slowly that their audience and team members are struggling to stay awake. This is not an effective way to motivate or engage with colleagues. It can create disconnection instead of a high-energy, vibrant work environment.

This section shows how to reduce the outward signs of high self-control if you feel your self-control is higher than is ideal for the work context you are in right now. It might sound odd to want to become more impulsive. A better word is spontaneous, and finding ways to be more spontaneous.

Do more of the following:

- Think about a strength you have and how you could use it the following day.

- Make decisions for yourself and make them right away.

- Make a list of all the small, medium and big things you want to achieve in life.

- Start doing a new thing every week – for example, if you do not talk to colleagues at work, make an effort to strike up a conversation every day.

- Lower your expectations. Identify what you, consciously or subconsciously, demand of yourself and others in social situations and then try to make them less intense and more realistic.

- When with other colleagues, do not think about what you are saying, just say it. Try to think less and express ideas as soon as they pop into your head. Do not wait to jump into a conversation, just jump in.

This will allow you to feel more at ease in social settings, open up more and enjoy conversations.

To further work on self-control, I recommend you consider going next to the skills and results areas highlighted in the map below.

EMOTIONAL RESILIENCE MAP **SELF-CONTROL**

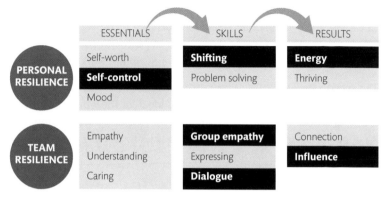

	ESSENTIALS	SKILLS	RESULTS
PERSONAL RESILIENCE	Self-worth **Self-control** Mood	**Shifting** Problem solving	**Energy** Thriving
TEAM RESILIENCE	Empathy Understanding Caring	**Group empathy** Expressing **Dialogue**	Connection **Influence**

Chapter **3**

Mood

'Mood is the background against which we work. It is the landscape against which our mind and body functions, and the foundations of our mental life.'

LIZ MILLER, BRITISH PHYSICIAN

This chapter will give you:

- an insight into how mood affects how you work and therefore your emotional resilience;

- two aspects to understanding mood, based on the past and the present;

- a way of distinguishing feelings from descriptions of states;

- a way to assess your own mood and decide what you need to be more effective in your current job (do you need to increase your mood or tone it down?).

Mood
Your emotional state at any given moment

Mood is the overall atmosphere that we create and then inflict on others through being with them, via our actions. Moods are not expressed directly, only indirectly through how mood influences our choices about what we do, say and think. It is a moment-by-moment awareness. Awareness of our moods enables us to live in the present, the now. Along with self-worth and self-control, this aspect of emotional resilience is absolutely critical, as it reflects the prevailing atmosphere at work.

To describe a mood, we sometimes use words like sad, mad, bad or glad. Though mood typically lasts much longer than a feeling, it indicates how in sync we are with what we are trying to do at work. Any unexpected happening can throw off our mood in a flash. Everyone around us is affected by our mood.

When we are in a positive mood, it has a multiplier effect. Many researchers have studied the positive impact of emotion. Fredrickson's broaden and build theories have shown that a positive mood is expansive and helps us to think more widely about a topic, whereas negative moods constrain our thinking. Typically, there are five things that affect mood – our surroundings, our physical body, relationships, knowledge about people and events, and our personality or nature.

Rottenberg's work on mood has been influential on my own understanding of mood. He describes moods as, 'internal signals that motivate behaviour and move it in the right direction' (Rottenberg, 2014). It is this sense that is most appealing to me in understanding mood for emotional resilience. In the descriptions that follow, whenever you see the word mood, try to think of it as a combination of thoughts, actions and feelings in the current situation you are in.

Practical observations

1. My observation is that, in business, many people have mood problems: just notice how people feel down at the slightest thing that happens. Our goal could be to be more neutral and to be able to use that neutrality to be effective. The self-assessment in this chapter is focused on that.

2. One very telling sign of mood is how a typical meeting takes place at your workplace. Is the mood positive, or is it constricted and negative?

3. Most people do not tune into the relevant activities that support their mood. If you are feeling very focused, then it would be a good time to attempt certain tasks. If you are sleepy and lethargic, then you may need to get some fresh air to make yourself more alert.

 WHAT YOU NEED TO KNOW

1. Twenty-two per cent of the population display at least one symptom of depression and the World Health Organisation projects that, by 2030, increased depression will have led to more worldwide disability and lives lost than any other affliction, including cancer, stroke, heart disease, accidents and even war.

2. Famous research investigated the connection between positive emotion and physical health and survival: a study of 180 catholic nuns, aged 75–95, was conducted through analysis of their handwritten autobiographies, which were created

▶

six decades earlier in the 1930s and 1940s when they were much younger and applying to join the convent (at the average age of 22). The stories were coded by researchers and graded as emotionally positive, negative or neutral. Researchers found a very strong link between positive emotion expressed through the nuns' stories and their lower risk of mortality. In other words, the nuns who lived the longest had expressed positive emotion through their stories and this direct link was found to hold for up to six decades of life. Sixty per cent of the least happy nuns died before the age of 80; the more positive nuns lived a decade longer than their more negative peers (Danner, Snowdon and Friesen, 2001). Follow-up studies included an analysis of the brains of the nuns who died, with over 500 brains donated for research on Alzheimer's disease. Researchers found that the positive nuns had no evidence of dementia symptoms, whereas the negative nuns showed evidence of dementia whilst still alive and in their brains after death. This provides evidence that negative emotions suppress the immune system and lead to illness and disease (Tomasulo, 2010).

3. The act of boosting our mood comes from doing what we intend to do, the things that are important to us (Pychyl 2013).

👥 MEET GEORGINA

I recently coached Georgina, who is a senior manager in healthcare. She felt that she did her job well, was ready for more responsibility and yet had been overlooked for promotion again. However, she also felt that colleagues did not seem to 'warm' to her, which she could not understand. She considered herself to be open and friendly and yet often she was not asked for advice or support.

Through coaching her, it seemed that her mood was at the root of her always pointing out negative things and this is what led to her shooting down everyone's ideas in terms of 'that will never work'. She thought she was just playing devil's advocate, but everyone else felt she was dismissing their opinions out of hand. This led to stakeholders not wanting her to be included in discussing ideas for new projects and her peers not wanting her support or negative attitude.

Georgina had not been aware that her mood was having such an unfortunate impact on her colleagues but, once pointed out, she could begin to see the problem. She began to be more sensitive to, and aware of, her mood and used reflection exercises. Her contribution to meetings improved and peers began to seek her out for advice. Three months later, there was the opportunity of a promotion and this time she was recognised as having more potential.

 Observe people at work who you consider to have a healthy mood:

- Who do you know who is infectiously positive and usually enjoys their life?
- Who do you know who smiles a lot and is fairly cheerful to be around?
- Think about these people and observe what they do to have fun during the work week and at weekends (you might have to ask them directly).
- Identify which aspects of this person's life you would like to have more of.
- Who do you know who keeps an upbeat mood and stays on top of situations, even when things get really tough?

- What language do these people use as reflective of their positive mood, even when things get difficult?

- What actions do they take as reflective of their reasonable confidence in accomplishing success?

- How do they plan for a positive result?

Use these questions to observe yourself:

- How do I feel when I am upbeat in my mood?

- What is the sensation in my body? (For example, bubbling in the stomach, need to shout out joyfully, warm feeling all over?)

- What do I do when I am in a good mood? (For example, smile more, laugh, talk more positively to others?)

- How does being in a good mood affect me in other ways? (For example, people behave differently towards me, I behave differently towards them.)

- What do I look like when I am in a good mood? What are my body language signs of a bad mood? (For example, breaking eye contact, tapping fingers or feet, waiting to interrupt, interrupting and breaking in.)

- What sensations do I feel in me when I exercise low or high mood? (For example, low mood: tightness in chest or shoulders, holding breath, gnawing in pit of stomach, rushing feeling in the mind.)

- How do I use optimism in my life? Do I use more optimism at home than at work, or vice versa?

- How do I feel when I feel optimistic? (For example, a feeling of lightness in the heart, a surge of excitement in the stomach.)

- What do I do when I feel optimistic? (For example, I speak more forcefully, with conviction; I move more quickly, I have a clearer sense of purpose.)

- What do other people say to me when I am optimistic or sound pessimistic?

Different moods for different tasks

It is true that we need different moods for different work tasks. To be effective in problem solving we might need to be more serious. To connect well with people, we may need to be more enthusiastic and upbeat. To learn effectively, we need to be relaxed and to have a sense of curiosity. So, when we talk about mood, we need to identify what overall combination of mind, body and sensations is most conducive.

A wonderful video, *Atmospheres*, illustrates the role of mood perfectly. There are two halves of the video, showing a businessman travelling across the Brooklyn Bridge in New York. In the first half, he is tuned in to all the chaos of the street sounds and the video makes you feel very unsettled and almost fearful as he drives past a number of awful street scenes. In the second half, the video has exactly the same images but with completely different music – this time you feel very peaceful as you listen to Pachelbel's Canon playing in the background. The same images look completely different with the contrasting music. This is a wonderful metaphor for mood: what is the soundtrack that we play in our minds through our emotional state while we work? Is our mood upbeat and positive or is it downbeat and negative?

 You can watch this video at the web link provided in the web resources.

Mood affects all interactions. It affects the atmosphere in which we do our work. It is a powerful build on our self-worth and our self-control, as it reflects how we actually feel in the moment. This, in turn, is likely to be a combination of our underlying mood (how we feel about our past, present and future), plus the mood we are currently in, based on our internal and external responses to the moment. This chapter focuses on these two core aspects. We will explore ways to shift mood in Chapter 7 Shifting. There are also some tips in Chapter 8 Problem solving, as the emotions we feel can give us useful signals about how we are doing.

How we feel about the past, present and future

Many of us will have a default mood that is a summary of our life and work experience that gives us a level of satisfaction with life. This natural mood that we emit to others will adjust up or down slightly, based on the current event or thoughts about a future event.

The complication with this essential is that our level of mood is deep-rooted in our early life, and many people think we require therapy to create a shift. Learning mood starts at birth and continues through inter-actions with our peers, parents and other adults through childhood and into adulthood. In a baby, mood is needed for learning rules and under-standing limits, though babies are not born with mood.

However, babies begin developing self-soothing skills – the beginning of mood – in their first months. For example, many babies learn how to soothe themselves by sucking on a pacifier or finger. This helps them cope with waiting and learning that they cannot always have everything they want. The good news about mood is that, with repetition, we can learn how to control ourselves – for example, at work, if we know that writing a to-do list is helpful for us to do at the start of each day in order to feel hopeful, but we struggle to make it a priority, then repeating the behaviour of writing a to-do list every morning is how to work on our mood.

A second aspect of mood is **the mood we experience right now and how it affects our behaviour.** It is helpful to be able to tune into our mood and there are some very useful tips that I will share with you later in this chapter. As adults in the workplace, some of us are very down at work and have a sense of depression, despair or hopelessness. The mind and body are closely linked, so it is not surprising to note that there can be health consequences of negativity.

The activities in this chapter cover both these aspects of mood.

Working on your mood

Mood affects not only what we do but how we do it. This is usually most apparent in times of high stress at work. It includes **what we do** (the action, for example, not talking to anyone because we are feeling down) as well as the **emotions we create in others** (for example, frustration, annoyance or support, encouragement) and **the outcomes** we experience (for example, success, failure). It also affects the way in which we interact with others (empathy, understanding, caring), which are covered in Part 1, and the skills that we need to use at work to be emotionally resilient, covered in Part 2 (emotion shifting, problem solving, expressing, group empathy, dialogue).

Working through the activities in this section will help you make a longer-term shift in your mood.

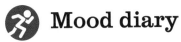 # Mood diary

This a very useful exercise for taking immediate action to change your mood at work.

Keep a feelings diary. Each day look back on the highs and lows, not just in terms of intellectual observation (for example, 'That was a good day'; 'That was a bad decision') but also in terms of emotions and sensations.

Examples include:

'That was a scary situation – I felt my pulse racing and my hands getting clammy.'

'I enjoyed giving that presentation. I was a bit scared at first, my stomach was full of butterflies but, when they said they would go with the project, I felt like bursting into song!'

'That was a very frustrating meeting. I could feel a headache starting, I was suppressing my yawns, I nearly fell asleep, I felt unstimulated – in fact, I felt a bit of anger there as well.'

Activities to improve mood

'I used to think that the worst thing in life was to end up alone. It's not. The worst thing in life is to end up with people who make you feel alone.'

ROBIN WILLIAMS, AMERICAN ACTOR AND COMEDIAN

Happiness is the experience of pleasant emotional states, directed primarily towards the present, rather than the past (life satisfaction) or the future (optimism). Happy people at work tend to be cheerful and feel good about themselves. Unhappy people at work tend to feel downhearted and can be overly negative about things.

Generally, people with low happiness tend to be disappointed with their life as it is at present. Optimism is how forward-looking you are and, if you view the glass as half-full or half-empty. Like happiness, optimism is linked to well-being, albeit in a forward-looking way. Optimistic people look on the bright side and expect positive things to happen in their life. Pessimistic people view things from a negative perspective. They are less likely to be able to identify and pursue new opportunities and tend to be risk-averse.

Think about pessimism: is it a character trait, a defect or evidence of incompetence? Find arguments for your point of view, then identify someone who is optimistic and debate this with them. Have a debate with someone else about whether there is a difference between realistic and unrealistic optimism.

One strategy at work is to try to be more neutral in your mood and to have a consistent mood. This can make a difference to the ups and downs of everyday work.

The activities in this section are:

- **Focus, openness and energy** – a daily scan of your mood.

- **Self-knowing** – knowing your feelings.

- **Optimistic reflections** – using everyday work events to note the positives.

- **Mood cost-benefit analysis** – assessing mood in yourself and others. This helps you to identify your key emotions under pressure, enabling you to decide what you need to change, so that you are more productive and true to your goals at work.

- **Neutralising mood** – how to cultivate a more even-tempered nature.

1. Focus, openness and energy

Use focus, openness and energy as a way to rate emotions in you and others.

On a scale of 1 to 10, where 10 is completely and 1 is not at all, calibrate yourself at the beginning of each interaction using the questions below:

F stands for **focus** (how focused am I feeling right now?)

O stands for **openness** (how open am I feeling right now?)

E stands for **energy** (how energetic am I feeling right now?)

Then, ask yourself, are these scores adequate for this situation?

If not... make an adjustment.

So, for example, if you lack:

Focus – try to remind yourself of the objective of the meeting and do not allow yourself to deviate from the discussion topic.

Openness – try to listen without prejudging, take on board other people's ideas and ask others what they think.

Energy – try to keep yourself hydrated and move around the room if necessary to get more energy.

When you are sitting in a meeting, in the middle of a task, or in conversation with someone, run through these questions on focus, openness and energy and score yourself on each dimension with a number out of 10, where 10 is high and 1 is low.

The more you consciously switch on this mode of self-observation, the more you develop your awareness of mood and how it affects how you work. Give yourself time, it may feel mechanical, clumsy and awkward at first but, with practice, it will become quick, easy and automatic.

2. Self-knowing

Learn core feelings to increase your confidence and repertoire for expressing feelings language in daily life. Eight common feelings are given below with a list of similar feelings words. The next time you use a feelings word, try to use the feeling marked in bold.

We will return to this later, but the key here is to be able to distinguish feelings from non-feelings.

I feel...

Happy	Scared	Sad	Confident
= core feelings			
Similar words not ideal for expressing feelings:			
alive cheerful content ecstatic exuberant grateful optimistic peaceful	afraid anxious apprehensive desperate insecure nervous shaken unsure vulnerable	distraught down empty hopeless sorrowful	capable confident effective hopeful proud secure self-reliant sharp strong
Try to avoid these –ed words:			
elated energised gratified	intimidated overwhelmed panicked terrified	alienated defeated dejected demoralised depressed disappointed disheartened drained resigned	accomplished assured determined encouraged

Excited	Upset	Angry	Tired
= core feelings			
Similar words not ideal for expressing feelings:			
alert curious energetic enthusiastic eager ready optimistic open cooperative	helpless stuck restless irritable futile uneasy	uptight upset hostile furious resentful mad	apathetic worn out numb empty weary weak vulnerable lethargic shut down
Try to avoid these -ed words:			
thrilled engaged involved stimulated connected	aggravated confused dissatisfied distressed frustrated hindered stifled	annoyed exasperated offended outraged humiliated betrayed agitated disgusted provoked	checked out disengaged exhausted fatigued stressed

3. Optimistic reflections

This is an everyday method of reflecting on your mood at work as regards your ability to consider positively the unfolding opportunities.

Step 1: Experience of optimism

Think of situations in your work, and in dealing with problems, where an optimistic attitude helped you or someone else. Note three examples. Be specific about who was optimistic in the situation, what they actually said or did, and what positive impact this had on the outcome.

EXAMPLE

> Expressed appreciation of teamwork
>
> Good feeling at start of meeting

You may wish to develop a daily practice of gratitude and keep a running list of what you are grateful for.

Step 2: My reactions to challenging problems

This activity is about reflecting on how you respond when confronted with an impossible problem and it encourages you to think about the positive value of the situation.

Think of all the times this month when something came up that was unexpected or not welcome. You might have thought, 'This won't work' or 'It's impossible' at the time. Write here as many phrases as you can think of that usually you used to reject the reality of the situation, and try to find a positive value in the situation to work on shifting your optimism in the face of everyday realities.

EXAMPLE

> Instead of, 'It won't work' suggest: 'It can work, let's find the right way to make it work.'
>
> Instead of, 'It's impossible' suggest: 'It's not the usual way of doing things, but let's see what we can do practically to make it a success.'

When procrastinating on a task, try to engage in projecting forward into the future to imagine the good feelings you will have after finishing a task and focus on these to help you get started on it.

🏃 4. Mood cost-benefit analysis

This activity is designed for you to assess mood both in yourself and in others. This includes your reactions under pressure so that you can be ready for the times when you need to show a more positive mood.

A template for this activity is available from the web resources.

1. Find three key words that reflect how you perceive yourself in your work.

2. Note them in the first column.

3. Then identify how you feel about your role and write this in the second column.

4. Then identify the costs of these feelings about yourself – for you, for your role, for your health.

5. Finally identify the benefits of these feelings.

6. Then do the same based on how you think others perceive your mood and look at the differences.

My current job example:

Qualities: how I perceive myself in my job in three words	Feelings: about my current job in three words	Costs: downsides of the feelings	Benefits: upsides of the feelings
For example: stressed over-worked people-oriented	For example: fearful sad angry	For example: I do not allow myself to believe I can change anything: my health; my enjoyment of life; my family time.	For example: I am good at understanding other people's bad moods. I get a lot done – fear drives activity.

▶

Qualities: how I believe others perceive my mood in my job in three words	Feelings: of others about my current job in three words	Costs: downsides of the feelings	Benefits: upsides of the feelings
For example: in control strong solid	For example: happy hopeful fear	For example: I do not really have a peer group. I may not be as approachable as I could be. No one really knows me well.	For example: People listen to me. People value my knowledge and the contribution I can make.

1. Now think about how you perceive yourself under stress. Go back over the lists and add any words that identify what happens when you are under pressure. It may be that the emotions you experience are different, so add these. If they are the same, circle the ones that are particularly present.

2. Finally, identify the emotions that are most counterproductive for you by circling the ones that have the highest costs.

3. Decide on actions to take to remove these costs and strengthen the benefits.

 You can download a book list on self-worth from the web resources together with some useful quotes that you can use as additional affirmations.

5. Neutralising mood

Try to distinguish between descriptions that simply state what happened (what, who, when, where) and interpretations that are judgements (feature words like bad, good, terrible, wonderful, should/should not).

Descriptions that are non-evaluative or neutral will lead you to feel more present in your body.

 You can access more examples of this important distinction within the web resources.

Further tips for achieving neutrality of mood are given below.

1. Imagine that everything that is difficult in your everyday work has a positive value for you.

2. Practise yoga – especially the postures where you breathe with an open chest; this has been shown to reduce depression and enhance mood.

3. Practise trying to see things from other people's perspectives.

4. In your everyday work, try to decide, on a daily basis, how to create the following three senses in your work: a sense of creating; a sense of freedom; and a sense of appreciation/gratitude.

5. Tune into your inner thoughts to work out what signal your mood is giving you and what you need to do differently.

6. Put situations into perspective. Be aware of your language and try to shift it from problem- to solution-oriented – for example, instead of saying, 'This is difficult,' try saying, 'We have a few challenges to work through.'

7. Be detached. Tell yourself that things do not really matter and most things will not really matter at all in six months' time. Say to yourself: 'This, too, shall pass.'

Quick tips for reducing mood

This section shows how to reduce the outward signs of raised mood, if you feel your mood is higher than is ideal for the work context you are in right now.

Do either more or less of the following:

- Think about a weakness you have and how it costs you a great deal of stress.

- Go back to the self-reflection activity on the six essentials ('Start point: self-reflection' in the Introduction) and remind yourself of all the descriptors of the negative impact of having a very high mood and identify where you can improve.

- From the analysis that you carried out earlier, you will be aware that some of the emotions you experience are created by you and some of them are the effects of your early life experiences. However, your response to what happens is directly in your control. Looking at this very simply, there are only three possible actions to take. The first two involve only yourself and the third involves what you do in relation to other people. Review each of the following questions and identify what you most need to do right now in your work.

Self: do I need to do more work on identifying what I really want from my job and my career, so that my mood can be better aligned?

Self: do I need to manage my own emotions to make the best of the talents I have?

Others: do I need to initiate a conversation with someone else (my boss, a colleague, a friend) to discuss:

- what is not working?
- what I would like to change, with their help?
- the benefits of this for both of us?

To work further on mood, I recommend you consider going next to the skills and results areas highlighted below:

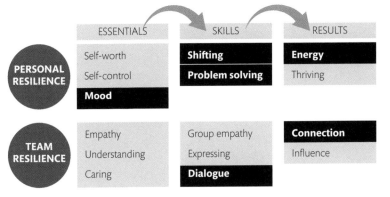

Having explored the self essentials, we will now move to the team essentials.

Chapter 4

Empathy

'A high degree of empathy in a relationship is possibly the most potent factor in bringing about change.'

CARL JUNG, SWISS PSYCHIATRIST AND PSYCHOTHERAPIST

This chapter will give you:

- insights into empathy and the art of listening for relationships at work;

- an introduction to an unhealthy set of behaviours called co-dependency, which can be confused with empathy;

- activities to try to increase your empathy.

Empathy
Tuning into other people's feelings so that you can take them on board when making decisions

Empathy is the extent to which you can enter the world of another person's feelings – to take a perspective from a different viewpoint of your everyday interactions. It is vital for building effective relationships at work. It involves imagining what another person might be feeling and responding appropriately. In other words, it has to do with whether one can understand other people's needs, perspective, desires and intentions.

People with healthy empathy tend to be skilful in conversations and negotiations at work because they take into account the viewpoints of those they are dealing with. They can put themselves in somebody else's shoes and appreciate how things seem to them. People who have challenges in empathy have difficulty adopting other people's perspectives. They tend to be opinionated and argumentative and may come across as self-centred. Too much empathy, on the other hand, can lead to feelings of emotional overwhelm.

The art of what is called 'generous listening' is very important here. I find that people who are genuinely very good at generous listening at work are able to hear both **what** is being **said** in words and what is **being communicated in non-words** – the colours, the energy and the movement that give you the true essence of how the person is feeling.

Many years ago I took part in a communication skills workshop where we had to listen to someone speaking about their problem for five minutes and then sum up their communication with us in one brief sentence. For example, 'So, you are feeling fearful about the situation,' or 'Quality is very important to you.' Then the person would give feedback on how accurate others were in describing the essence of their experience.

One of the tools I have learned in the last few years is to actually say the words, 'I hear you' when someone is expressing a feeling, or 'I hear you are angry.' Very simple and very important, but not common in business.

There is also an aspect of our being – how we are being with others as opposed to what we know or what we do. Bringing an atmosphere of personal humility and compassion in the presence of listening to others will help us to connect well with others.

There is also the role of ego and whether or not we are able to put ourselves out of the conversation in order to be fully present and tune into someone else. Being perfectionistic about our relationships is impossible and risky, as there is so much that relies on the uniqueness of human interactions. Having empathy relies on being able to go with the flow of another person.

Connecting with others can fill us up in a very positive way and is an essential part of work. There is no joy better than having a meaningful connection with colleagues we work with. I find that connections at work really are the fabric of what matters most in work. Empathy is about being in a positive relationship with our colleagues.

> **'When people talk, listen completely. Most people never listen.'**
>
> **ERNEST HEMINGWAY, AMERICAN AUTHOR AND JOURNALIST**

Dr Paul Ekman, a well-known pioneer in the study of emotions, has classified all emotions into eight categories and has promoted the importance of teaching the skill of recognising emotions through facial micro-expressions, brief flashes of emotion in a fraction of a second.

Teresa Wiseman (a nursing academic) studied a wide range of professions where empathy is relevant. She came up with four qualities of empathy – perspective taking (recognising the other person's perspective as their truth); staying out of judgement; recognising emotion in others; and communicating that to others.

The web resources include a link to a TED talk by Dr Helen Reiss on empathy.

Practical observations

1. People at work who struggle with the Essentials described earlier (self-worth, self-control, mood) will have difficulties building true empathy with others.

2. Empathy can go too far very easily and become enmeshment, an unhealthy family dynamic where a person becomes a surrogate spouse or parent for someone else in their family. I have seen this happen in teams where a person becomes overly attached to someone and the working relationship is unhealthy. It is useful to know the difference between empathy and enmeshment.

3. Empathy makes a significant impact on how you feel when you are working with colleagues; it is the difference between wanting to work with someone and not. Empathy is obvious when you observe two people interacting; are they really **seeing** each other or not?

WHAT YOU NEED TO KNOW

1. Research following 60 employees over 2 weeks in an IT company found that managers who showed empathy were able to generate a climate of understanding and support, which boosted the well-being of their team members. Those who experienced more empathy from their managers, whether about a positive or negative situation, were also less likely to report feeling sick and were happier after making progress towards goals when compared with people whose managers were less empathetic (Scott et al. 2010).

2. Through 40 years of research, it is possible to learn how to recognise emotion through facial

---

expressions. Recognising emotion is the first step in building empathy.

3. Empathic accuracy is usually good in relationships, where you can hear accurately how the other person is feeling. In the relationship of a couple, when things are going badly, continued lack of empathic accuracy is associated with irreparable damage (Flury and Ickes, 2006).

MEET HANNAH

When I met Hannah, I noticed immediately that she had a very welcoming and caring nature and it was easy to recognise what a good mentor she was within her multi-national company. In this spirit, she had wanted to contribute something to her local community and so had offered to lead some adult literacy classes as a local volunteer.

However, from our discussions, it was soon apparent that, rather than just teaching she had been drawn into the problems of particular students and was almost taking on the role of a remote carer: helping with day-to-day problems such as contacting utility companies or the banks about issues the student did not feel confident in tackling. She started to worry too much about the people she was tutoring: the old lady whose husband used to do everything in connection with the house, but has since died, leaving her feeling vulnerable and paralysed with fear; the Egyptian man whose English wife had died tragically during an operation and now worried about his grasp of the language; and the teenager who had failed at school, but could restore a vintage motorbike and needed to build some self-confidence and have his skills acknowledged.

Hannah needed to learn to take a step back and realise that empathy is a positive ability to tune into another person and notice how they are feeling, but that she was becoming co-dependent, where empathy goes too far and where she was becoming absorbed into other people's needs to the detriment of her own.

I worked with her on setting some healthy internal and external boundaries where she could take charge of how she allowed other people to interact with her; still expressing empathy and compassion but maintaining her own well-being without being emotionally overloaded.

Empathy – *is being able to put yourself into someone else's shoes.*

Emotional overload – *is what happens when empathy goes too far and you start to feel totally flooded with emotion.*

Compassion – *the ability to be able to tune into the suffering of someone else, but to stay in an adult mindset where you can have understanding but without the flood of emotion.*

 Observe people at work who you consider to have healthy empathy:

- Who do you know who is good at understanding the way other people feel?

- Who do you know who genuinely sympathises with other people's plights without being too involved?

- When you see this person with others around them, how do they show their sensitivity and awareness of other people?

  - Is it mainly through their words?

  - Or through gestures or non-verbal communication?

  - Or through their actions?

- Give examples of what you notice.

Use these questions to observe yourself:

- When people are talking to you, how do you show you are listening? For example, what is your body doing? Are you making eye contact, is your expression showing attentiveness, is your stance open and receptive? What is your mind doing? Are you trying to put yourself in their shoes, feel their feelings, and have their thoughts?

- Are you distracted easily by electronic gadgets – phone, tablet, etc?

- When talking to others, do you tend to translate what the other person is saying into your own words so you can understand them better? If you do this, are you judging whether what they are saying is right, acceptable, or correct?

- What do you notice about other people when they are talking to you? Do you look at their expression? Do you notice their body language? Can you detect their emotional state?

- When you respond to what someone else is saying, do you show you have understood them by paraphrasing it back?

- What do other people say about your empathy skills? What do they observe about you? For example, 'They notice I always look at them when I am speaking and they get the feeling I really want to understand them,' 'I don't rush them,' or 'They get the feeling I am just waiting for them to finish so I can say what is on my mind. It's really irritating!'.

Co-dependency and boundaries

It is essential to distinguish empathy from co-dependency. Empathy is a positive ability to tune in to another person and notice how they are feeling. Co-dependency is empathy gone too far: when you become totally absorbed in other people's needs and then forget your own.

It is my belief that our workplaces are full of people who are unhealthily co-dependent. They put others' needs before their own and then end up unhappy, disengaged and burned out.

One of the keys to having good relationships is to have healthy internal and external boundaries. **Internal boundaries** allow us to control and to take responsibility for our own thoughts, beliefs, opinions, feelings and rights. These are ours and we do not blame others for things that we do not have. We take note of our own values, reactions, opinions, memories, decisions and behaviours and use these to be in healthy control of our own lives. We do not focus on the other person's feelings, decisions, behaviour, time, bad habits, wants and dreams.

External boundaries are what give us control over our physical being. We are in charge of who interacts with us and how they interact with us. If we are not good at setting boundaries, we become a victim of other people's unhelpful behaviours.

Co-dependency destroys healthy relationships.

One of the activities later in this chapter focuses on behaviours of co-dependency.

So how, then, do we show healthy empathy?

Working on your empathy

Working through the activities in this section will help you to make a longer-term shift in your empathy.

1. Emotion barometer

This exercise involves choosing someone to follow in order to track their emotions. Follow a colleague through a typical day and plot their highs and lows through the day as a curve on a graph, showing how high they are feeling versus how low. Name their emotions when you can – how they change and what triggers the changes. Follow your own emotional state as you observe throughout the day: your own highs and lows and what triggers them (these could be associations with current and previous life events). Once you have done this a few times, try to differentiate between other people's emotional states, to fine-tune your empathy barometer.

WWW You can download an example from the web resources.

🏃 2. Connected listening

Practise being fully present so that you connect with the other person and offer your generous listening.

When you find yourself quick to judge someone, suspend your judgement until you have sought some common ground.

1. This means practising more listening, with the only objective being, 'Do I really understand what motivates this person? Do they experience me as a good listener?'.

2. Look for opportunities to find common ground that might be outside of the current agenda – for example, common interests, hobbies, etc., and build rapport on this platform first.

3. Examine alternative options for yourself to prevent you from using your passion and energy in a negative way – for instance, instead of getting angry and frustrated with someone who you experience as not being straight, authentic or genuine, perhaps you could channel your emotions into compassion and tolerance, 'I can see they are not being themselves – this must be difficult for them, they would be a much better person and more at ease with themselves if they could be straight and genuine with me. Perhaps, if I show them tolerance and compassion, this will help them to be more like themselves.'

4. Conserve your energy in difficult interactions by checking how well you understand their point of view, 'Let me get this right – so, what you are saying is that you want xyz, or you seem to be feeling abc. Is that accurate?'. There is no point in moving forward the discussion until you have understood fully their position and they feel your acknowledgement of them.

5. Ask people how they are feeling. 'OK, John, so we are agreed that this is the right course of action, but what I really want to know is how you feel about it. Does it excite you? Are you a bit apprehensive? Or does it feel boring?' When you relate to people on a feeling level you are helping them to be genuine with you.

6. If someone shares something very difficult with you, consider saying, 'I don't even know what to say right now, I am just glad you have told me.'

3. Observatory

This a very useful exercise for learning to be an observer of others – a people watcher, noticing reactions, language, styles of communication, rather than wondering what you will say next. Practise saying nothing in meetings if you are someone who would usually jump in with your views and opinions. Or, instead of giving your views and opinions, make it your goal to show, by rephrasing what other people have said, that you have understood the contribution of others.

4. Top 10 empathy tips

Here are some practical suggestions for how to work on your empathy, if you believe that your empathy is lower than ideal for your work goals.

Do more of the following:

1. Ask others how they feel – on a scale of 0 to 10 – and make eye contact when doing so. Use your own awareness to recognise others' feelings. Make an effort to be more sensitive and understanding of others. You could also ask, 'What would help you feel better?'

2. Avoid saying, 'You need to; you have to; why didn't you; you should; you shouldn't; you should have; you shouldn't have.'

3. Improve your listening ability by giving others the opportunity to express themselves completely, without interrupting, judging or trying to solve their problems. Listen to the whole person and do not judge until you have all the information. Put your mobile phone away and tune into the person you are with. When you are in a conversation with someone, keep a constant check on what you are thinking and what you are feeling. Pay attention to how much you are focusing on yourself and how much you are tuning in to them.

4. Improve your ability to read body language. Tune in more to non-verbal communication. Tone of voice changes occur when a person is feeling upset, so listen out for these. Use your posture to signal an open approach to others.

5. Remember that the muscles of human expression are in the face. Pay attention to emotions in people's faces.

6. Learn the tools of the HeartMath system to help yourself to regulate emotion, particularly the tools of heart-focused breathing, inner ease, quick coherence (heart focus, heart breathing and heart feeling) and freeze frame (freeze the moment, quick coherence, heart-focused problem solving).

7. Learn to appreciate differences in people, validate and empathise with them without getting infected, i.e. feeling responsible for the cause of a problem or solution and getting drained.

8. Test the correspondence between what you experience and what objectively exists. Notice when you are speaking *facts* and when you are expressing *feelings* and notice how different the reaction is in the other person.

9. Try to label the feelings of the person you are talking to, by putting an emotion label to the feeling you are hearing. Practise reflecting others' thoughts and feelings. Paraphrase their thoughts or ideas and reflect back their feeling messages, 'So, what I am hearing is that you feel angry...'

10. Recognise how you feel when someone shows concern for you and how it makes you feel when you show concern for someone else.

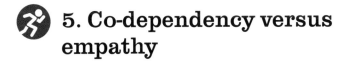 5. Co-dependency versus empathy

This activity focuses on the difference between co-dependency and empathy, which it is useful to clarify. However, while empathy promotes effective communication and mutual respect, co-dependency destroys the foundation of healthy relationships, as it involves a pattern of thinking, feeling and/or behaviour where you cannot tell where you begin and others leave off. It is not helpful for relationships. Co-dependency can even be considered an attempt to control others.

Here are a few questions to ask yourself to determine if you are acting with empathy or co-dependency. Of course, the distinction is not always so clear-cut. It is likely that there are many moments in your day when you are acting with both: your empathy intention might evolve into meeting a need of your own. An awareness of your actions is key to keeping towards empathy and away from co-dependency.

1. What are your intentions? To alleviate suffering or self-protection?

When we move beyond the emotion of empathy to actively want to alleviate another's suffering, our intention might be motivated by selflessness. The underlying motive of co-dependency, on the other hand, is that of self-protection. The co-dependent person wants to be needed and is pursuing acceptance and safety. S/he often takes on the role of a martyr or a victim, and makes it about him/herself. In that way, co-dependent activity, although seemingly charitable, is closer to selfish than selfless.

2. How do you feel, emotionally and physically? Lacking connection or good?

Because co-dependency is a form of relationship addiction, it generates the hangover feeling that most addictions leave you with and deteriorates emotional and physical health. Empathy, on the other hand, promotes general health and well-being. In fact, recent studies show that empathy makes us feel good in a variety of ways. It activates pleasure circuits in the brain, secretes the happy hormone oxytocin, slows down our heart rate, makes us more resilient to stress, and boosts our immune system.

3. Do you value the other person more than yourself?

Both empathy and co-dependency may involve attending to others' needs. At times, this requires personal sacrifice. However, a compassionate person continues to care for him/herself in the process; s/he never abandons her/himself in order to take care of another. A co-dependent person, on the other hand, discards his or her own needs, replacing them with the needs of the other person. Then s/he becomes bitter, resentful, and frustrated when there is nothing left for her/him at the end of the day.

4. Do you feel like you have a choice?

Co-dependent persons do not have a choice in taking care of another person, or at least they feel as though they do not. There is an exaggerated sense of responsibility, a fear of abandonment by the other person if they do not pull through. They are not performing free acts of charity as a compassionate person does. They are imprisoned by a sense that something terrible will happen if they do not attend to another's needs and do whatever they need to do to enable behaviour, even if they acknowledge that it is destructive.

5. Is the relationship healthy?

Empathy strengthens the relationship. Acts of selflessness contribute to mutual appreciation, effective communication, trust and other key ingredients of successful relationships. Co-dependency, on the other hand, deteriorates the foundation of relationships, causing jealousy, bitterness, destructive behaviour, poor communication, and a host of other problems. Co-dependency usually is found in relationships that were dysfunctional from the start, where one or both people are involved in destructive and addictive behaviour.

6. Do you feel guilty?

Unlike empathy, co-dependency is associated with an overwhelming feeling of guilt. Guilt is often the motivating factor for decisions and behaviours within the relationship, even though they do not make any logical sense.

Tip for reducing empathy

Many of our workplaces emphasise collaboration and teamwork but you want to be sure that you are not tuning in to others' needs, feelings and perspectives more than is healthy. Co-dependency is what happens when empathy goes too far and you start to take on the feelings of another person.

To avoid this happening, try the following:

Remind yourself that the feelings belong to another person. Taking on those feelings is a lot like carrying someone else's emotional baggage. In work, often we have to deal with other people's baggage as well as our own. By taking on another person's feelings, we are adding to the baggage we already have. At some point, we can become too weak to carry anyone else's, so we need to return it to them and let them carry the baggage themselves!

To further work on empathy, I recommend you consider going next to the skills and results areas highlighted below:

EMOTIONAL RESILIENCE MAP **EMPATHY**

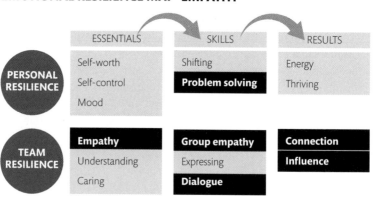

	ESSENTIALS	SKILLS	RESULTS
PERSONAL RESILIENCE	Self-worth Self-control Mood	Shifting **Problem solving**	Energy Thriving
TEAM RESILIENCE	**Empathy** Understanding Caring	**Group empathy** Expressing **Dialogue**	**Connection** **Influence**

Chapter 5

Understanding

'Understanding changes perceptions. The greater the
understanding, the truer the perception.'

ANONYMOUS

This chapter will give you:

- an insight into how to get to know your colleagues better and how this contributes to your personal resilience;

- a clear description of five social needs that affect how people work and the opportunity to reflect on how well these needs are met at your workplace;

- a checklist for getting to know your colleagues in the right way, so that you can know what is essential for you to work well with others;

- upfront understanding about the things that annoy you or other colleagues you work with, so you can be better prepared for likely areas of tension.

Understanding

Tuning into what colleagues need in order for them to be effective at work

Understanding in a work context is about being aware of your colleagues and their work styles, including strengths and weaknesses, attitudes and views, skills and interests, concerns and needs, personal circumstances that might affect how they work, and aspirations, so that you can work together effectively and achieve positive results. It includes being able to understand the needs, perspectives, skills and feelings of team members.

When understanding is strong in a team, it builds safety and trust. Research shows that it is a strong predictor of performance in a team (Druskat and Wolff, 2015). One of the outcomes of a high-performing team is that the team is able to be resilient in the face of pressures. Understanding contributes to that.

In a team context, understanding each other has been found to be among three team behaviours that are most linked with outstanding performance in a team (team researchers Druskat and Wolff). Knowing your colleagues and how to work with them is not soft; it is a hard factor, essential for being able to know how to work together.

Events can be a trigger for accumulated emotion or unprocessed emotion.

In a recent example, two colleagues ended up having a big argument about something very small. Some anger can be triggered by situations not relevant to the current one, so being understanding requires us to keep our side of the street clean and not be drawn into other people's unresolved hurts.

Practical observations

1. It is very easy in a team to make incorrect assumptions about what people are thinking and the intentions behind their behaviour. In a team recently, I noticed that one team member continually scratched his knee and left the room whenever his boss spoke. This was not ideal for the interaction. The instinctive judgement I made was to believe he was a difficult personality. Through working with the team and noticing that no one challenged him leaving the room on three occasions, it became clear that there was something he did not feel able to express to the team and this was creating some internal frustration. Once this was understood and he could express himself, he stayed in the room and was very much part of the dialogue.

2. Many team leaders do not allow sufficient time for the team to get to know each other. I am not advocating big outdoor adventure team-building sessions, but spending time getting to know each other (with some of the structured activities mentioned here). This enables people to bring their best emotions to work and to work through the inevitable difficult feelings that can arise in a team.

3. I am constantly surprised at how little people bother to find out about other people and how much better the enlightened leaders are, who are able truly to understand their team members. When I work on consulting projects, often I ask managers what they know about their team members outside of the work environment. Frequently they look blank or make something up, which is often untrue. Usually they have never asked the questions.

⚙ WHAT YOU NEED TO KNOW

1. Psychologist Susan Fiske has discovered that we have five social needs that affect how we think, feel and behave in social situations. They influence our ability to perform at our best in social groups. The needs are belonging (this one is the core need), understanding, control, self-enhancement and trust (Fiske, 2004). The satisfaction of these needs makes it possible to function effectively as part of a work team. These five needs are included in two of the exercises in this chapter.

2. Disclosing personal information can help to build understanding within a team, but research shows that it is not necessary. What is important is for team members to have a solid understanding of the unique skills and knowledge that each person brings to the team. You do not need to like your team members to be able to understand them. This is a very important distinction and tip. The purpose of understanding people is not to know the intimate details of their lives, but to know enough about them to anticipate their unique needs and perspectives and work well with them (Druskat and Wolff, 2015).

3. Mentalisation is the ability to see ourselves as others see us, and to see others as they see themselves. This is a technical term for accurate understanding and the ability to avoid misinterpretations. Stress impacts this process and makes it difficult for some people to interpret actions accurately; stress is considered to be linked with early life experiences of secure or insecure attachment (Fonagy *et al.*, 2002).

MEET KATE

Kate was working for a top executive in a very male-dominated environment. In her role, it quickly became apparent to her that there was a very clear divide between 'us', the admin staff (mainly women), and 'them', mainly men dealing with large sums of money and with seemingly even bigger egos. The women felt they were perceived as a financial overhead rather than actually being very necessary to the firm. Consequently, they felt there was a lack of appreciation for their roles, which enabled the company to function. Extra work was done grudgingly, leading to a lack of respect on both sides. Kate was nominated to approach the CEO and other executives about resolving the situation.

It was found that neither side had a clear understanding of the other's job role or importance within the business. The perceived lack of praise and appreciation had not been intended, it was just that everyone was too wrapped up in their own lives to notice colleagues or to try to gain a better understanding of each other. Due to the gender imbalance on both sides, female staff had found it difficult walking into a large room full of men, but it turned out that the men were also uncomfortable approaching the women with additional work.

Over the next six months, both sides were actively encouraged to find out about the everyday stresses and activities in each other's roles and gain a deeper appreciation of the value of each person to the business as a whole. Praise and thanks were offered in a genuine and sincere way, when deserved, on both sides. Turnover and staff absenteeism decreased significantly.

 Observe people at work who you consider to have a healthy understanding of their team members:

- When working in a team and assigning roles and tasks, what questions do they ask to find out about strengths, weaknesses, skills, interests and personal pressures?

- Which open questions do they use to find out more about an opinion opposite to their own?

- How long do they persevere with trying to understand the other person, when asking questions?

- How do they reflect back the perspective of the other person?

Use these questions to observe yourself:

- When someone disagrees with you, what do you do typically?
- How easy do you find it to suspend evaluations of the person before you hear or understand their point of view?

Basic needs

Susan Fiske identified five basic needs and it is very useful to note how these are built into our everyday work and to learn in which areas of our work we feel fulfilled and unfulfilled. The needs are:

- **Belonging:** people are motivated to connect with and bond with each other. Sometimes this is simply the feeling of being respected in a team so that you actually want to be part of that team. You feel part of a family and want to belong. Without belonging, it is impossible to feel trust in the team.

- **Understanding:** means that you feel the need both to understand people in the team and to feel understood by them. This removes feelings of self-doubt and shame.

- **Control:** is the motivation and desire to influence how work is done and to feel in control of decisions about the work. This creates a sense of initiative and removes guilt over ineffectiveness at work.

- **Self-enhancement:** is the motivation to feel that you are socially worthy and can take actions to improve yourself in the team. This gives a feeling of both efficiency and effectiveness at work.

- **Trusting:** is being able to trust team members and be trusted by them. This enables you to contribute in a valuable way without suspicion or a need to control others.

Working on your understanding

Working through the activities in this section will help you to make a longer-term shift in your understanding of colleagues.

'Deep understanding is the most precious gift one can give to another. Everything that irritates us about others can lead us to an understanding of ourselves.'

CARL JUNG, SWISS PSYCHIATRIST AND PSYCHOTHERAPIST

🏃 Reflection: social needs

This exercise involves reflecting on your basic needs and the extent to which they are met in your role. Also use them to decide on actions to take to help others to reach their core needs.

Rate each of these needs on a scale of 0 to 10 to indicate how well each need is met in your current job.

	Me in my role	A close colleague in his/her role
Belonging	0–1–2–3–4–5–6–7–8–9–10	0–1–2–3–4–5–6–7–8–9–10
Understanding	0–1–2–3–4–5–6–7–8–9–10	0–1–2–3–4–5–6–7–8–9–10
Control	0–1–2–3–4–5–6–7–8–9–10	0–1–2–3–4–5–6–7–8–9–10
Self-enhancement	0–1–2–3–4–5–6–7–8–9–10	0–1–2–3–4–5–6–7–8–9–10
Trusting	0–1–2–3–4–5–6–7–8–9–10	0–1–2–3–4–5–6–7–8–9–10

Activities to improve understanding

When working in teams, there is a variety of ways to get to know each other. Four activities included in this section are:

- **Knowing each other** – five key questions to find out about every team member.

- **Facts, values, aspirations** – a useful way to build understanding of your team members.

- **Understanding areas of difficulty** – identifying what annoys you and others.

- **Behaviours in meetings** – a checklist of behaviours to demonstrate understanding.

1. Knowing each other

This activity helps to build trust in a team by encouraging discussion with each team member about themselves and their hopes for the team.

- What do others need to know about you and the way you like to work?

- What do you hope and expect from people in this team?

- Is there anything you find challenging about working in teams?

- We all have 'hot buttons' (things that make us upset or angry). What are some of yours?

- What are your greatest hopes for this team as a whole?

2. Facts, values, aspirations

The following activity is based on helping others know you and on developing more flexibility in how you deal with the emotional content of your job. It is designed to make it easy for you to get to know the people you are leading. By being open about yourself, you free others to want to share their own background with you.

Step 1. Write down the following information about yourself:

- Facts: where you live, what you do for a living, your educational background, your family background, your hobbies.

- Values: what is important to you in terms of family, friends, how you live your life?

- Aspirations: what are your important visions, dreams, goals in work and home life?

Step 2. The next time you meet with your colleagues or your team, tell them this information.

Step 3. Invite others to do the same. In a team, you might want to use a table like the following one to find out more about the other colleagues you work with.

Names	Facts	Values	Aspirations
	Examples: where they live, what they do, educational background, family background including number of siblings and birth order, hobbies, past jobs, experience in the sector or company, biggest challenge in job so far.	What is important to this person in terms of family, friends, how they work and how they live their life? An important challenge in their childhood or in their careers that might have provided important learning or insights into how to be effective in work.	What is important to this person in terms of their vision, dreams, goals in home and private life?

In order to succeed with Step 3, you will need to be very upfront about why you are asking people in your team to share this information. Tell them it is to make everyone aware of the backgrounds and experiences represented within the team.

3. Understanding areas of difficulty

Following on from Chapter 2 Self-control, not regulating emotions can not only get in the way of relationships but also damage them forever. This activity encourages you to return to your 'hot buttons' – things that other people do that annoy you, terrify you, that lead to you losing your cool or having very negative thoughts. In this activity it is recommended that you identify how you would handle these 'hot buttons' in others and the actions you choose to understand in order to move forward. There are three steps involved. I encourage you to complete them now.

Step 1. Return to the situations that annoy you, frustrate you, terrify you or anger you about your work.

Step 2. Now rank these by adding a number next to each one to identify the frequency with which you experience each one in other people – ranging from 1 (least frequent) to 10 (most frequent).

Step 3. Now identify which need is not met in you and then have a conversation with a colleague about this, to identify their perspective on what you could do.

Step 4. Plan to have a conversation with your manager or your stakeholder to discuss ways of working that can enable you to get your needs met. As part of this conversation, go through each of the five needs and find out how you can help them.

Sometimes the other person is your direct manager and this activity is designed to help you to build understanding and have a productive conversation about things that annoy or irritate you both.

If you need inspiration to kick-start the process, here are some examples.

Situations	Rank	Reason behind it
People reacting to being nagged – particularly being told the same thing twice within five minutes	3	Need for understanding
People reacting to me not doing what I say I am going to do	5	Need for trusting
People reacting to me being late for things that I have committed to doing	4	Need for control
People not having enough free/social time together	1	Need for belonging
People reacting to me working hard to meet deadlines when everyone else has gone home	2	Need for self-enhancement

Hopefully this will create more understanding of other people you interact with.

 # 4. Behaviours in meetings

This activity focuses on a checklist of ways to demonstrate understanding in a meeting. Use it to stay on track.

1. Start a meeting with a brief feelings check – ask how everyone is doing on a scale of 0 to 10 and give each person a minute to say how things are going and how they are feeling. If someone says 'fine', ask them to say more. If someone's score is very low (for example, a 0 to 2), then ask the person to express to someone else later what is going on, if it is too personal to discuss in the meeting. If it is something about team performance and is not about an individual's performance, it is right to talk about it in the meeting, as long as the team has created some ground rules for engaging with each other.

2. When you encounter an unacceptable behaviour, ask why and try to find out what is behind the behaviour. Ask questions and listen.

3. Encourage team members to give their full attention to each other in meetings. Ask people in the meeting to put aside their phones and notebooks and tune in to the person who is speaking.

4. If someone says something you do not fully understand, or if they have an opinion that is different from yours, keep asking questions until you understand them.

5. At the end of every meeting, ask if anyone wants to add any comments.

By consistently including these in every meeting, you are likely to start being proactive about building understanding.

To further work on understanding, I recommend you consider going next to the skills and results areas highlighted below:

EMOTIONAL RESILIENCE MAP UNDERSTANDING

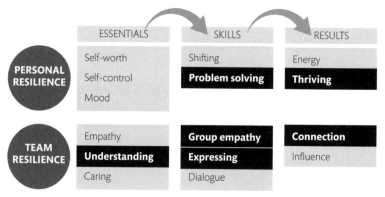

	ESSENTIALS	SKILLS	RESULTS
PERSONAL RESILIENCE	Self-worth Self-control Mood	Shifting **Problem solving**	Energy **Thriving**
TEAM RESILIENCE	Empathy **Understanding** Caring	**Group empathy** **Expressing** Dialogue	**Connection** Influence

Chapter 6

Caring

'No one cares how much you know, until they know how much you care.'

THEODORE ROOSEVELT, US PRESIDENT

This chapter will give you:

- an insight into the additional value of caring on top of empathy and understanding;

- a clear description of caring behaviours in a team;

- the distinction between validation and invalidation and how this helps you to be effective, working as part of a team;

- practical actions to build trust in a team;

- an opportunity for reflection on how you contribute to each colleague you work with, to help you focus on more actions you can take to increase your level of caring.

Caring
Showing that other people matter so that colleagues are able to make their best effort at work

Caring is how much you treat others with kindness and respect. It includes showing concern through the way you support other people's needs and efforts. In a team where people value, respect and support each other, there is a feeling of compassion between individuals beyond empathy and understanding.

Caring is one of the behaviours that indicates an outstanding versus a mediocre team. Teams improve their performance by 25 per cent when they work on team emotional intelligence (Druskat and Wolff, creators of team emotional competence theory, 2015). Caring behaviours are part of team emotional intelligence.

 You can access further information on this framework via the web resources.

People in teams can care for each other even when there is conflict. The interesting thing is that we do not even have to like one another or socialise together to care about each other. Caring is not a behaviour that happens solely when colleagues socialise outside work. Caring can be shown by anyone in a team to a colleague, a visitor or a stakeholder. It transcends hierarchy and authority. Usually it involves frequent actions rather than one-off behaviours, a series of small things that add up to a warm feeling over time – a thank you, a brief acknowledgement of a job well done, recognition, a helping hand through tough moments.

Caring is also visible in moments of conflict. This can involve seeing the other person's perspective and acknowledging it, having an accurate understanding of why they reached the point in the conflict and taking a positive step to let them know that you care about them. If a team member is being attacked, caring means not tolerating rudeness, disrespect or discourtesy from another team member or from others.

A caring behaviour in a time of disagreement means showing concern for your team member, even when they are angry with you or when they disagree with you. It involves accepting the moving reality of work in teams, that we are all changing, that we all constantly make mistakes, that we all have differences in perspective, which can be helpful.

Whilst hard to do sometimes, in these tough moments it is about taking an action to engage the person more and to talk about their hopes and fears, rather than leaving them out in the cold. Caring is also associated with listening and drawing in quieter members of a team. In times of uneven workload, it might involve you helping a team member before an important deadline when they are overloaded.

In short, caring is about doing what is right by the people in the situation, not what is easiest.

Practical observations

1. Caring actions can be as simple as a compliment, a thank you or appreciation for something that helped you. It sounds simple, but is not common in every workplace.

2. In teams where people are skilled in displaying caring behaviours, often you hear people being drawn into meetings – 'Who haven't we heard from? Who else has something to add? What other perspectives are there on this problem?'.

3. In some workplaces, I am sorry to say that I have observed a shocking

absence of caring. I remember visiting the site of a well-known company to present some research findings. The meeting room we were using had to be used for emergency resuscitation for an office employee who had fainted. This brought out some visible signs of frustration in a few managers in the meeting who were annoyed that the paramedics had to use our meeting room. This is what I would call completely unlimited uncaring.

4. Focusing on goals and being caring do not have to be mutually exclusive in a work environment. I find that the organisations that have both usually are the most successful in their sector.

⚙ WHAT YOU NEED TO KNOW

1. Research with top management teams identified that the single most important factor in predicting organisational performance was the ratio of positive statements to negative statements during interactions. This was more than twice as powerful as any other factor. In high-performing organisations, the ratios were 5.6 positive statements to 1 negative statement. In medium-performing organisations it was 1.85 to 1 and in poor-performing organisations 0.36 to 1 (Vanette and Cameron, 2009).

2. Expressing gratitude regularly is associated with better physical health, optimism, progress towards goals, well-being and helping others (Emmons and Crumpler, 2000).

3. A 1990 study by Robert Baron (Ryback, 1998) found that 'negative or critical feedback was considered a greater source of conflict and frustration than disputes over power, mistrust or personality struggles'. Criticism kills a part of the person; affirmation builds. The complication here is that, if someone's behaviour at work necessitates negative feedback, then how do we handle it? Everyone cannot always receive positive feedback. The point here is that we have to make sure that our feedback is caring. (This is given focus in Chapter 11 Dialogue in the section on giving feedback.)

MEET YASMINE

Someone I had the pleasure to work with has been a perfect role model for caring. Yasmine has been leading a team for many years in different organisations. When you see her work station, it is covered with photos, personal gifts and lovely quotes. All these are gifts that she has been given by other colleagues and people close in her life. Why? She invests a great deal of her energy in saying thank you and in remembering and marking people's special days (birthdays, anniversaries). As she has become busier, she has become more successful yet she has not lost this central quality of caring for others and showing people she cares. She is rare in business. The small touches of caring really do make a big impact on how others feel about working with us.

Observe people at work who you consider to have a healthy caring attitude:

- What questions do they ask others, if they want to show caring in the team?
- How frequently do you observe caring behaviour in your workplace?
- Which actions seem to have the most impact on others?
- How often does the team leader display caring actions?

Use these questions to observe yourself:

- When you write emails at work, how do you typically start and end them?
- How easy do you find it to carry out acts of kindness for your immediate colleagues at work and for your boss?
- When was the last time you did something altruistic for people in your team? What did you do and what was the positive impact?

 # Validation

One of the keys to emotional resilience for teams involves the ability to differentiate between validation and invalidation. Let us start by defining these words.

Validation means acknowledging, accepting, understanding and nurturing people and their feelings – it involves accepting someone's individuality. When the chips are down, very often all we need is to feel validated. When things are normal at work, we appreciate hearing how much other people value us. I am frequently surprised to see people literally grow an inch or two during meetings when you give them a compliment. This is not common in workplaces but could happen more frequently.

Invalidation is acting in a way that rejects, ignores, mocks, teases, judges or diminishes someone or their feelings. Invalidation goes beyond mere rejection, by implying not only that our feelings are disapproved of, but also that we are, fundamentally, abnormal. Invalidation is one of the most counter-productive ways to try to manage emotions. It kills confidence, creativity and individuality. Telling a person they should not feel the way they do feel is akin to telling water it should not be wet, grass it should not be green, or rocks they should not be hard. Each person's feelings are real. Whether or not we like or understand someone's feelings, they are still real. Rejecting feelings is rejecting reality; it is fighting nature and may be called a crime against nature, psychological murder, or soul murder. So, you can see why it is so frustrating, draining and futile.

In teams, particular forms of invalidation take place. Sometimes it can involve keeping people in the dark about their performance, or using personal attacks, sarcasm, angry tones, and the like. Such behaviour usually elicits one or more of these reactions: defensiveness, tension, antagonism, people making excuses or avoiding responsibility, people ignoring the leader and, ultimately, people leaving the organisation.

Working on your caring

The activities in this chapter cover a few different aspects of caring.

Working through the activities in this section will help you to make a longer-term shift in your caring.

Reflection: building trust

This exercise involves reflecting on each of five characteristics in a strong relationship and deciding which ones need further effort in each of your work relationships.

Start by listing what each word means to you, then identify how it can be shown in the form of a caring behaviour within the team.

	What it means to me	How it can be shown in my team
Truthfulness		
Respect		
Appreciation		
Support/validation		
Listening		

 You can download a template for this activity from the web resources.

Activities to improve caring

There is always something that can be done to increase the level of caring in a team. The activities in this section are ways to do this.

- **Validation and invalidation** – a way of distinguishing your caring and uncaring behaviours in a team.

- **Contribution to team members** – thinking about each person and what you can do specifically to be thoughtful towards them.

- **Caretaking versus caring** – how to make sure that you do not start being over-caring and move into caretaking.

- **Everyday work tips** – suggestions on how to communicate caring through email communications and texts.

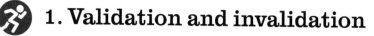

1. Validation and invalidation

Think about how you behave in the team that you work in. Put a tick next to all the items that are typical of you – if possible, check this out with a colleague.

My behaviours working in a team: validation		My behaviours working in a team: invalidation	
I accept, understand and nurture other people's feelings.		I tell others they should not feel the way they feel.	
I acknowledge and accept other people's unique identity and individuality.		I dictate to others not to feel the way they feel.	
I allow other people to safely share their feelings and thoughts.		I tell others they are too sensitive and too dramatic.	
I reassure other people that I will still accept them, even if they share their thoughts.		I ignore others.	
I reassure others that it is OK to have the feelings they have.		I judge others.	
I let other people know that I respect their perception of things.		I lead people to believe there is something wrong with them for feeling how they feel.	
I help other people to feel heard, acknowledged, understood and accepted.		I reject people's individual identity.	
I listen and show my agreement non-verbally (for example, I nod).		I am a poor listener – I have too much mental chat going on when I am supposed to be listening to other people.	
I am patient when others are not ready to talk.		I am impatient and often tap my hands and feet and fidget.	
I offer to listen.		Often I do not offer to listen to other people's views, particularly when feelings are involved.	
I am present both physically and emotionally with other people.		I find it hard to stay in the present and stay focused on what someone is saying.	
Total number of validation:		**Total number of invalidation:**	

2. Contribution to team members

Ask yourself what specific contribution you can make to every single person who works with you and take steps to make this happen – express this to them as a commitment and use this activity to exert personal leadership alongside your practical or technical expertise.

Name of team member	Contribution I can make to them

3. Caretaking versus caring

Use the description below to remain mindful of times when you might step into caretaking, which is when caring becomes too much for the situation and works against your own needs. This destroys working relationships.

There is very little room for negative feelings in our workplaces because the typical unwritten rule at work is, 'It is not OK to feel.' So, we suppress our feelings whilst inside we might be upset. Then, to handle this, the human way is to act as if everything is fine because another workplace rule is that we have to be strong, independent and self-reliant. Better not show our vulnerability.

So, naturally, when someone bursts and falls apart, sometimes it is usual to want to go to the rescue (whilst others run away). But this is not necessarily because we care. Many of us come to the rescue because we cannot bear to see someone else experiencing difficulty. So we help them in order to reduce our own discomfort. And, others of us come to the rescue to get approval and validation from our colleagues and stakeholders at work.

If you can relate to this and feel the personality of a caretaker inside you, think about it in your own work. When a colleague is struggling, does the caretaker in you mobilise and assume your struggling friend needs something – some practical help, or support of some kind, and do you take it upon yourself to rescue, help or save the day? Or are you able to stay centred and support them in a healthy way?

There are three primary reasons you will caretake:

1. The fear of feeling uncomfortable watching someone else suffer (feelings of discomfort).

2. The fear of losing the working relationship if you do not help in time (feelings of loss).

3. To seek and gain the approval of people whose opinions you value, for example, your boss (feelings of likely gain).

Let us look at an example. Many people, when they were young, if they did not caretake their parents, then they were easily rejected, abandoned, shamed and even humiliated. When they did things that helped to care for others, but went beyond care to caretaking, they were rewarded with praise and approval for being a good little boy or girl. As adults, if we risk not caretaking, and instead are willing to be ourselves, we might feel the childhood fear of losing a relationship, so we do not say what we want to say to be sure not to upset the other person. So, to trust that you will be OK with an uncomfortable feeling and able to speak your truth goes against everything I learnt as a child.

Thus, emotional resilience involves learning how to care for someone, whilst also still holding my self-worth, so that I can handle my own discomfort and genuinely be there for my colleague, whilst not needing anything in return.

Here is a helpful distinction between caretaking versus caring for someone:

Caretaking: trying to make someone feel better because you want to be liked by them, or your desire to help them is coming from your own fear/discomfort and your desire to get rid of the uncomfortable feelings in yourself when you see them in a difficult situation. The underlying message you are sending is something like, 'I don't trust that you can take care of yourself. You need me and my help.' This can prop you up and make you feel valued by being such a caring person. You get some validation by giving and you enjoy that, even to the point of feeling proud. The other person ends up feeling like something is off in the interaction. The caretaker is out of touch with their own needs, so indirectly they get their unmet needs met through giving.

Caring for: helping or serving someone because genuinely you feel care for them. You trust that they do not need you or your specific help, but you feel called to be there for them. You do not lose yourself in your caring of them. In fact, you do not even need to do anything (although you might) because how you feel inside sends the message of 'I accept you through this.' They end up feeling held and cared for by you.

Check yourself on this one. Next time a colleague at work is challenged, notice your response. Do you want to rescue them? Do you feel called to help because you want to silence the discomfort going on? Do you get a quick hit of approval having offered yourself to them?

Last, what is the cost of your caretaking behaviour? Are you, actually, less available to your friends and loved ones because you are so busy taking care of everyone? And, how are you with receiving support? Do you let others help you out or are you always the helper? Any resentments there?

If we want to learn a new way to care for someone, it helps to understand why we caretake. What drives this behaviour in each of us and is it really serving us and those we care about? Once we understand our motives, and the cost of our behaviour, we have the power to choose a direction that is in alignment with what we want out of work.

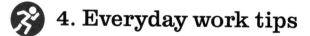

4. Everyday work tips

Emails

Here are some suggestions on how to communicate caring through simple email communications and texts.

The following examples give you sentences from the beginnings and ends of emails. You may wish to review them and note the subtle changes to make them appear more caring.

EMAIL

Hi All

I wanted to send a quick reminder out for our September meeting, which will be held on **Wednesday, September 24th at 10am EST**.

MORE CARING VERSION

Hi All

Hope this email finds you all enjoying the last part of Summer.

I wanted to send a quick reminder out for our September meeting, which will be held on **Wednesday, September 24th at 10am EST**.

EMAIL

Alex

A colleague suggested that I contact you and I hope that you are able to point me in the right direction.

MORE CARING VERSION

Good day, Alex

Hope this email finds you well. It has been a while since we connected and I am looking forward to hearing your news.

Someone suggested that I contact you and I hope that you are able to point me in the right direction.

Small things

> 'If you take care of the small things, the big things take care of themselves. You can gain more control (...) by paying closer attention to the little things.'

EMILY DICKINSON, AMERICAN POET

Here are some suggestions on small things at work that can make a big difference:

- Ask, 'Is everything OK?' when you see a colleague looking mad, sad or bad. Do what is right by the people in the situation, not what is easiest. Recognise people's efforts for something they did well. Say thank you. Show care to visitors by welcoming them and providing them with what they need (water, tea, snack).

- Do kind things for no reason at all. For example, point out someone's strengths; bring flowers to work; offer to buy a colleague lunch; bring fresh fruit to share; be public when it is a celebration (for example, a birthday); help a team member when they are overloaded before an important deadline; show caring to stakeholders by hearing their needs.

- Communicate one-to-one with a person when there is something difficult in their life, to show you care (health problem, struggles with financial debt, or a death in the family, for example); offer a listening ear; give a colleague a hug when they are down (if appropriate to your relationship with them); give someone a helping hand through tough moments.

- Develop greater objectivity about any difficult colleagues (for example, who are angry or critical). Show concern for your team members, even when they are angry with you or when they disagree with you. Imagine what might be difficult in their own lives or what might be making them unhappy or angry. See the bigger picture. Build a deeper understanding of your colleagues. See the other person's perspective and acknowledge it. Accept that we are all changing; that we are all making mistakes all the time; that we all have differences in perspective, which can be helpful. Have an accurate understanding of why they reached this point in the conflict. Remember that your team members are not just a number; caring behaviour in a team will have a payback to the team.

- Do not tolerate rudeness, disrespect or discourtesy from another team member or from others. Remember that better understanding and caring between team members makes your work life much richer.

- Draw in quieter members in a team in meetings when they have not said anything. In times of conflict, make a concerted effort to engage the person more and to talk about their hopes and fears, rather than leaving them out in the cold.

- If you do not have a process in your team at the moment, suggest a process that enables everyone to hear each other and hear what is going on in their work and what the issues are. Some teams will start their meetings with each person saying in one sentence how things are going right now.

To work further on caring, I recommend you consider going next to the skills and results areas highlighted below.

EMOTIONAL RESILIENCE MAP **CARING**

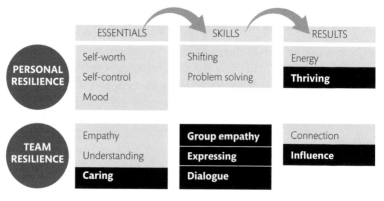

Part 2

The Skills

The **skills** are the practical steps you can develop to overcome challenges arising from the **essentials**.

Having discovered the six essentials and, hopefully, having read the chapters relating to your priority essentials, now you are ready to learn and practise skills to help you be emotionally resilient. These skills enable you to take action, no matter what challenges you face with the essentials.

With the skills, the question is: 'How do I adjust myself to handle difficult emotions?' This involves being able to solve people problems effectively when there is emotional content.

You will learn five skills that will help you to take appropriate action in work situations when you are feeling emotionally challenged.

Sometimes it involves making a shift in your emotional state. In teams, it involves expressing your thoughts and feelings effectively so that others can hear you clearly; tuning in to the feelings of the group and, finally, initiating conversation when things are not going well.

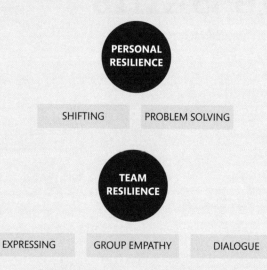

Each of the five skills is related to how we use emotion in the workplace. Learning to use these skills effectively can increase our effectiveness and performance at work.

1. **Shifting** your emotional state, so that you choose the emotional state that is most suited to what you are doing and your desired outcome.

2. **Problem solving** the emotions that arise and using the emotional data on emotions to make a decision on what to do next.

3. **Expressing** emotion effectively, so that others can hear you clearly, particularly when something is difficult or not going to plan.

4. **Group empathy** involves reading the feelings of people in a group situation and deciding whether the emotions are constructive for what you are trying to do.

5. **Dialogue** about the emotions that come up, including giving feedback on the situation.

Chapter 7

Shifting

'Shift your attention, and your emotion shifts.'

FREDERICK DODSON, AMERICAN AUTHOR AND TEACHER

This chapter will give you:

- clear evidence that your emotional state matters for your performance at work;

- reflective work to focus on longer-term aspects of emotion shifting;

- an understanding of the importance of being able to tune in to how you are feeling physically through practising a body scan;

- tools and tips for shifting your emotional state in the moment, including tools of being present and recalling moments of pure enjoyment;

- an insight into the triggers of emotional reactions at work and what action to take when you experience strong emotions.

Shifting
Changing your emotional state in response to everyday events

The definition above has three components: to make a **conscious decision** about your emotional state; to do this **immediately**; and to meet your **needs** in the situation you face. The decision to shift is driven by realising that how you are being is not helpful and consciously choosing a different emotional state.

Perhaps we are anxious or feeling angry at a colleague and want to create more calm before we can tackle our work again? For some people, shifting emotions means being able to change unpleasant moods, like feeling moody or irritable. For others, it is about noticing that your thought patterns have run away with you. Learning how to make a shift is useful for preventing an 'amygdala hijack', where our emotional brain reacts and causes us to do or say something we regret later. Imagine that a colleague asks if they can speak with you privately, or your boss calls you to a meeting unexpectedly. What do you think about naturally? Do you carry on and just have the conversation, or do you allow yourself to create a whole number of possible scenarios – is your colleague about to resign her job? Is your boss about to give you bad news?

When you are in a state of high anxiety, anger or gloom (see Chapter 1 Self-worth, Chapter 2 Self-control and Chapter 3 Mood), it is natural to fall into some unhealthy thought patterns. Your thinking might get carried away as you imagine a series of soap opera events that have not even occurred. You begin to make things up in your head and you imagine the worst scenario. You make snap judgements and can come to the wrong decision if you do not have the self-control or self-worth to stop yourself. You might blame the people around you and feel like a victim.

So, what can you do when you recognise that you need to make a shift?

If you are hungry, angry, lonely or tired, you may need to take care of yourself and watch how much energy you put into fighting others. Our physical bodies can have a big impact on our emotional state. If you are overly serious and stuck in a thought pattern, you may need to move physically, laugh or bring about a spirit of playfulness.

The first step is being able to realise that what you are feeling or thinking is not working for you in the moment, and this requires you to be tuned into your emotional state at all times. Whilst shifting refers mainly to an immediate or short-term change in your feelings and emotional state, by doing this repetitively, you are likely to make a shift for the medium- and long-term in your everyday routines for how you handle your emotions at work. Consequently, you will feel more fulfilled and happy at work.

People at work who are able to make these shifts are more likely to be able to pick themselves up after emotional setbacks at work and stay resilient. They can overcome periods of prolonged anxiety or even depression. They can stay nimble and make good decisions on the spot.

A key point here is that I am recommending shifting as a positive and healthy shift in emotions. I am not advocating that we repress our emotions, hide them or numb them through alcohol, caffeine or any other harmful substance. I suggest you take a moment several times a day to stop and check how you are feeling.

Practical observations

1. Many people in the workplace seem to accept their feelings as a given, so this notion of shifting emotions may be unusual for some readers.

2. Your total environment at work, including your physical working conditions, your relationship with your team members and your boss, can have an impact on how you feel. Depending on your workplace, it might be harder to shift your emotions or you may need to do this more frequently than is ideal.

3. Being effective in any work context requires you to shift your emotions, as your goal is to stay focused and grounded and ensure events do not throw your self-confidence or ability to get your work done.

4. Personally, I find that when a person is feeling very stressed at work, it can be extremely helpful to engage in an activity that requires 100 per cent attention using the more creative side of the brain. For example, I have a list of songs that I recommend clients download from iTunes and use to shift their state.

 You can download this list of songs from the web resources.

⚙ WHAT YOU NEED TO KNOW

1. Research shows that, when neural pathways in the brain are lit up during the experience of a disgusting event, these are exactly the same pathways that are lit up when an experience of something disgusting is recalled. In other words, the memory of an actual experience generates an identical set of neural pathways in the brain as the actual experience. This is a key reason why the skill of shifting emotion is vital as, without it, we can hold the memory of events as if they are still happening, even when the actual experience occurred a long time ago (Carter, 1999).

2. Various studies examined the impact of positive emotions on physical and mental functioning. The HeartMath Institute asserts that our capacity to self-generate a positive emotional state and quickly shift to a physiologically coherent mode at will can be developed and refined. Shifting is, therefore, a skill worth learning.

In this chapter, I am going to share with you two initial reflection activities, as these can be very important for understanding your underlying feelings at work in more detail. This will make a start in tuning in to your actual emotions, so that you can shift them when necessary:

- Is your career safe?

- High life low life

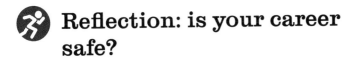 # Reflection: is your career safe?

This is a reflection on your underlying feelings at work and will help you to review the feelings that you experience at work now. You may be employed or self-employed. You may be working in a largely technical, managerial or administrative role. You may be part-time, full-time, employed or contracted. This review will help you get more in touch with the feelings that you are experiencing right now – the emotions covered are acceptance, sadness, anger, fear and enjoyment.

Review each of these feelings categories and identify the feelings that you have in your current job. Circle a number in each line.

1. Acceptance – a theme of bonding

How often do you experience the following?

	Never	Sometimes	Often	Very often	Always
Camaraderie with team members or other colleagues	0	1	2	3	4
A positive relationship with a particular person	0	1	2	3	4
Receiving recognition or a promotion	0	1	2	3	4
Praise for a job well done	0	1	2	3	4
People noticing the detail of what you do well	0	1	2	3	4

2. Sadness – a theme of helplessness

How often do you experience the following?

	Never	Sometimes	Often	Very often	Always
Actions being beyond your control that arouse strong emotions	4	3	2	1	0
Work or project undertakings that are changed later by management	4	3	2	1	0
Failure of another person or project affecting me	4	3	2	1	0
Restructuring or redundancies	4	3	2	1	0
Dull work environment	4	3	2	1	0

3. Anger – a theme of injustice

How often do you experience the following?

	Never	Sometimes	Often	Very often	Always
Others criticising you	4	3	2	1	0
Your suggestions or comments being ignored	4	3	2	1	0
The organisation/employer acting in an unfair way	4	3	2	1	0
Others not being productive	4	3	2	1	0
Tight deadlines/heavy workload	4	3	2	1	0
Dealing with angry members of the public/customers	4	3	2	1	0
Lack of cooperation from others	4	3	2	1	0
Stupidity/ignorance of others	4	3	2	1	0
Not being treated respectfully	4	3	2	1	0

4. Fear – a theme of uncertainty, especially about your actions

How often do you experience the following?

	Never	Sometimes	Often	Very often	Always
Your own failure to carry out tasks	4	3	2	1	0
Threats to job continuity in the present position	4	3	2	1	0
Threats to survival at an organisational level	4	3	2	1	0
Threats from your supervisors	4	3	2	1	0
Threats from your customers	4	3	2	1	0
Not expressing your fears to your supervisor/manager	4	3	2	1	0
Threat of an industry downturn	4	3	2	1	0

5. Enjoyment – a theme of success

How often do you experience the following?

	Never	Sometimes	Often	Very often	Always
Enjoyment from the work itself	0	1	2	3	4
Positive actions from your superiors	0	1	2	3	4
Positive actions from your peers or subordinates	0	1	2	3	4
Praise from your supervisors	0	1	2	3	4
Fun at work	0	1	2	3	4
Laughter	0	1	2	3	4

Add up your scores. If you have a score that is between 85 and 128, consider yourself lucky.

If you have a score of between 43 and 84, you may want to discuss with your manager what can be done to make your career happier (see Chapter 11 Dialogue).

If your score is below 43, you may want to ask yourself serious questions about whether this is the right job for you and what you might need to do to shift your emotions for the longer term.

Reflection: high life low life

This is a reflection on the major events in your work life so far. Review your career and identify five high points and five low points. You may wish to draw your career as a line to show the highs, lows and plateaus. For each of the high and low points, identify what was happening at work and the key feelings you had about self, life and others. Separate the feelings that are serving you well from those that now are obsolete (but may still be part of your daily functioning).

 You can download an example of this activity from the web resources.

MEET SUSAN

Susan is the leader of an 11-person team that delivers services through a regional network of advisers. She asked me to coach her to help overcome self-confidence issues following a major personal trauma that left her barely able to work. Susan recently has returned to work and has a key stakeholder, Rachel, with whom she is working to gear up for a high stakes, delicate meeting in three months' time from the start of our work. The catalyst for Susan to seek coaching is her desire to be functioning at her best and emotionally resilient at the forthcoming meeting and to take steps to sustain recovery from her recent personal challenges.

When we first talked about emotional resilience coaching, Susan was experiencing an extremely challenging time; she found it difficult to focus even on the conversation. I felt her level of anxiety and pressure about the coaching and her everyday life; I heard her need to find immediate solutions. With a crucial meeting coming up, Susan was despondent, largely concerning the strong likelihood of a negative outcome that would damage her confidence and career. It was clear from the outset that the impact of the coaching would have a lifelong effect on Susan. She feared that if she was not 100 per cent well and fighting fit, she would produce a negative outcome. Learning how to shift her emotional state was absolutely vital for Susan to improve her self-confidence. Susan practised the exercises in this chapter, recognising that her feelings of low self-confidence were not helping her. She needed to learn to shift these emotions for her own survival.

We discussed how the skill of shifting could influence her emotional health, her perceived work–life balance conflicts, and relationships with others.

 Observe people at work who you consider to have strong skills in shifting:

- How do they sound? What words do you hear them use to shift their emotions?

- How do they appear to you? What do you imagine they actually do to shift themselves?

- What aspects of how they are would you like to demonstrate more in yourself?

Use these questions to observe yourself:

- Are you aware of emotions at work that are holding you back?

- Can you identify choices you are making in your expression of emotions and your behaviours?

- Are they leading to your own health and happiness?

- Do your work colleagues promote positive thoughts or negative, limiting ones?

- Do you believe in your ability to shift your emotional state?

- In which situations do you find it most difficult to shift your emotions? (Situations when you are, for example, angry, sad or fearful? Situations with a particular person or group of people?)

- When you do not regulate your emotions, what are the adverse consequences of this in your interactions with others?
- How does this affect the overall outcomes/results you desire?

Body awareness

Your emotional state will reflect itself in your body so, if you are feeling sad you might slump. This also works in reverse. In other words, your body and posture influences your emotions. It also follows that you can choose the body posture that is going to help you feel a particular emotion. This is an important strategy in shifting your emotions. There are two different ways of doing it. A **full body scan** involves bringing awareness to your entire body and is a useful exercise to do often, as part of building up awareness of your feelings in the body. A **brief body scan** is a short version to do at work when you are feeling triggered.

 There is a recording of these two sequences that you can download from the web resources.

Full body scan (5 minutes)

- Take a deep breath in... Check your neck – is it straight? Is it leaning to the side? Tensed? Try to even it out and relax as much as you can. Move your neck gently from side to side.

- Now move to your shoulders. Are they uneven? Do you pull them forward? Do a few shoulder rolls back and forth. Notice how that feels better.

- Take another deep breath in. Check your back... Is it straight? Do a brief stretch. Hold your arms in front of your chest and pull them forward, bend your back all the way back. Stretch your back out. Now, pull your arms behind your back, holding them together, pull your chest forward.

- Take another deep breath. Now put both your feet down, rooting them firmly in the floor.

- Now take a deep breath in, close your eyes. Listen to your body. What do you feel? Is there a slight pull in your body?

- Take another deep breath in. Relax. Relax your jaws. Let them drop slightly. Relax the tensed muscles of your forehead.

- Listen. Listen. Listen.

- Notice if there is somewhere else in your body where you can detect a pulling or grasping sensation. Scan your entire body and notice how far this sensation spreads. What parts of the body compensate for it?

- Deeply breathe into these tensed muscles. Keep doing this to open up. This allows you to access the deeper memories of your unprocessed emotions, which can slow us down in our everyday work life.

Brief body scan (60 seconds)

When you sit, stand or move, or talk to someone close to you, try to notice all of the different physical sensations in the body:

- the head;

- the neck;

- the back;

- the chest;

- the arms;

- the hands;

- the stomach;

- the legs – thighs, knees, lower legs;

- the feet;

- the way you are standing/sitting/moving – as if you are a fly on the wall.

Tools for shifting

We will now turn our attention to how to shift emotions.

Working through the tools in this section will help you in your shifting ability long-term. These tools have been used with hundreds of clients and have helped to make a permanent shift.

There are three tools included here for shifting your emotions at work:

- **being present;**
- **Recalling moments of pure enjoyment;**
- **hot buttons.**

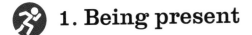 1. Being present

This is a tool that you can use at any time when you need to make a shift. As soon as you notice that you are reacting emotionally, follow these four steps:

1. **Relax** – breathe and release the tension in your body.

2. **Detach** – clear your mind of all thoughts.

3. **Breathe** – drop your awareness to the centre of your body just below your navel. Feel yourself breathe in and out of your centre. This helps to clear the mind. Ideally, do square breathing (breathe in for a count of 4, hold for a count of 4, breathe out for a count of 4, and hold for a count of 4).

4. **Focus** (and implant) – choose one key feeling word that represents how you want to feel in this moment and repeat it to yourself, 'I am feeling (new feeling).'

You might want to also consider the following steps:

- Learn mindfulness as a way to be in touch constantly with your emotions.

- Tune in to how you are feeling in the moment using the following – on a scale of 0 to 10, how **focused** do I feel? How **open**? How **energetic**? If you are feeling lower than a score of 5 on any of these, do something to change your state.

- When you are in an interaction with someone, keep a constant check on what you are thinking and feeling.

- Develop best and worst case scenarios. One way of doing this is to play devil's advocate with yourself and, when appropriate, with others.

- Test the correspondence between what you experience and what exists objectively. In particular, notice when you are speaking facts and when you are expressing feelings.

- Ask others to check with you on how you are feeling.

- When you develop an opinion about something or somebody, collect feelings-related information to understand what the underlying emotions are.

- Sharing your thoughts and feelings may help you gain more objective insights – ask for feedback.

2. Recalling moments of pure enjoyment

This tool involves actually recalling and re-experiencing a positive feeling. In 60 seconds, you can shift an emotion, change your physiology, and become more effective and happier. Your body is capable of responding in just a few breaths. The key to being able to do this is to practise holding the experience of these memories. This is a learnable skill. Then when we need to shift our emotions, we recall this feeling. This is based on a technique called Heart Lock-in created by the Institute of HeartMath, which I have adapted here.

Remember times when you felt really happy. For example:

- you were with people you love;

- you were recognised publicly at work;

- you were on holiday, in a favourite location, you can re-experience all the smells, sights, sounds and tastes;

- you were speaking to a friend on the phone and sharing recent news and laughing together;

- someone told you they care about you and you felt warm all over.

Now close your eyes, recall these times and hold these happy feelings for as long as you can. Some people find this useful to do with pleasurable background music. If you think it might help, find some music that is conducive and set aside a few minutes a day to generate positive emotion.

I use this technique when I go to meetings with clients and it works to completely shift my emotional state, no matter how stressed or pressured I felt a moment earlier.

I would recommend that you learn the entire suite of tools from the HeartMath system as part of mastering how to shift emotion, particularly the tools of neutral (heart focus and heart breathing), quick coherence (heart focus, heart breathing and heart feeling) and freeze frame (freeze the moment, quick coherence, heart-focused problem solving).

3. Hot buttons

'The ultimate measure of a man is not where he stands in moments of comfort and convenience, but where he stands at times of challenge and controversy.'

MARTIN LUTHER KING

This tool involves identifying all the things that get to you at work.

When your brain perceives a threat, real or imagined, then your emotions are triggered. You react with anger or fear and you may lose trust in your boss or the work situation. You may lose courage or react in a way that could hurt team relationships in the future.

A useful step is to notice when your emotions are triggered. Remember that needs are not bad, however. The more you are attached to these needs, the more you will be scanning your environment for circumstances that threaten your ability to have them met. Then your needs become emotional triggers.

At some point, you will need to make a decision about the situation. Is this a real unmet need or not? Is a colleague or your boss actively denying your need or are you taking the situation too personally? If it is true that someone is ignoring your need or blocking you from achieving it, can you either ask for what you need or, if it does not really matter, can you let the need go?

If we honestly declare our needs – that we had expected people to treat us in a particular way and had hoped events would unfold as we had planned – then we can begin to see things more objectively. From this perspective, we are freer to choose our reactions.

Not shifting your emotions can not only get in the way of working relationships but also damage them forever. This activity encourages you to identify your hot buttons – things that other people do that annoy you or cause you to have very negative thoughts. In this activity, identify the frequency of these hot buttons and the action you choose to take to move forward.

The following list includes some of the most common emotional triggers, meaning you react when you feel as though you are not getting or will not get one of your important needs met. This links back with the basic needs that we met in Chapter 4 Empathy. Some of these needs will be extremely important to you. Others will hold less emotional meaning for you.

Start by identifying up to five of these hot buttons that are usually triggered in you when you do not get your needs met.

For example, absence of:

- autonomy;
- belonging;
- understanding;
- control;
- self-enhancement;
- trusting;

- being treated fairly;
- freedom;
- fun;
- new challenges;
- respect.

Step 1. List the recurring situations when you don't get your needs met.

Step 2. Now rank these by adding a number next to each one to identify the frequency with which these occur – ranging from 1 (least frequent) to 10 (most frequent).

Step 3. Now identify what you need to do about each one:
- forgive the other person or people in the situation;
- forget about it;

- discuss it and express your view;
- acknowledge that you need to change something, otherwise the relationship will deteriorate;
- accept this as a part of your deeply held values.

Sometimes the other person is your direct manager and this activity is designed to help you to have a constructive conversation about how your needs can be better met.

If you need inspiration to kick-start the process, here are some examples.

Triggers Lack of...	Situations	Rank	Action
Autonomy	Being told what to do	7	Discuss
Control	Being nagged – particularly being told the same thing over and over again	4	Discuss
Consistency/ being valued	My colleague not doing what they say they are going to do	8	Forgive/ accept
Order	Colleagues being late for every deadline	5	Discuss/ accept
Self-enhancement	Colleagues relying on you to do the things you do not want to do	6	Forgive/ discuss
Being included	Not having enough social time together	1	Acknowledge
Balance	Working hard to meet deadlines when everyone else has gone home	2	Acknowledge
Balance	Not enough holidays	10	Discuss

Now that you have identified the hot buttons in your work relationships, those that you need to discuss or acknowledge require a conversation that provides equal time and space to air your and the other person's view so that you can try to reach a middle ground. From my experience, many problems can be resolved just by identifying the areas of difficulty. They cause a shift in us from being burdened with a problem to knowing how to resolve it.

Chapter 8

Problem solving

'This idea that decisions are made based on lots of rational facts is wrong – you take decisions based on 25 per cent of available facts.'

MARTIN TAYLOR, JOURNALIST AND BUSINESSMAN

This chapter will give you:

- an understanding of how to use emotions as data;

- the distinction between core feelings and behaviours, states and judgements;

- tips for self-soothing; a very effective coping strategy when you feel strong emotions;

- an insight into how to work with each core emotion;

- a five-step method for tuning in to your feelings;

- a process for setting working expectations so that you can create a culture for using emotion;

- tips for dealing with differences and disagreements.

Problem solving

Resolving problems of a personal, emotional or interpersonal nature by tuning into emotions as data

When most people think about problem solving they think about problems of a practical or rational nature. The problems that require us to be emotionally resilient are the problems involving personal or interpersonal tensions. This is when we need our emotion-based problem-solving tools.

The definition above is completely relevant to emotion problem solving. I advocate that we use an analytical approach consistently, the only difference is that the content of our problem solving is emotion.

Having these tools available enables you to get straight to the problem. The outcome is productive working relationships, healthy conflict and peace of mind.

Some of the tools in this section require you to think differently about how problems occur and what to do about them. Sadly, many people in the workplace do not have tools readily available for solving problems involving people (which covers most of the problems you will meet).

Effective problem solving involves being able to use emotions as data to assist us to find the right decision for a work-related problem. Few of us have been taught to do this, but these are learnable skills and ones that can provide many new avenues of potential solutions.

Through the earlier work in Part 1, you have started to identify the patterns in yourself that need work, if you are going to be emotionally resilient. You are now ready to learn some practical tools to make a shift in your effectiveness.

Practical observations

1. A large number of problems are caused by people not being able to be honest about what they feel and need. These are key steps in being able to use emotions as data – speak your truth and state what you need.

2. Using emotions as data is a new mindset for business. Most people tend to ignore emotions as irrelevant. Yet all the neuroscience research points to the reality that emotion is data and shows up in our brains.

3. Our level of emotion-based problem solving is a significant factor in how we build emotional resilience in the workplace. Therefore, it is the first skill on which to spend time.

 WHAT YOU NEED TO KNOW

1. It is well established in research that emotion accompanies problem solving but it is not researched in depth.

2. One of the earliest researchers, Herbert Simon (1967), claimed the need to develop a general theory of thinking and problem solving that incorporates motivation and emotion. Simon considered emotion and motivation as the two instances that control thinking by interrupting the system and allowing the processor to respond to urgent needs in real time.

▶

3. The physical composition of emotions has been studied. Researchers have found that they are represented in the physical form of neuropeptides and receptors, known as the biochemicals of emotion; these are messengers, carrying information to link the major systems of the body into one unit that we can call the body-mind. We can no longer think of the emotions as having less validity than physical, material substance. Emotions are at the nexus between matter and mind, going back and forth between the two and influencing both (Pert, 1997).

MEET HILARY

Recently I helped Hilary, who has continual work-related issues. She has had problems keeping a job due to dyslexia, and her work relationships always seem to deteriorate quickly. Her self-confidence and self-worth are very low and, now, with each job she tries, she expects to fail. She now takes this negative mood and low expectations to all jobs she starts. She is always fearful and emotional about a new role and there is also a sense of guilt and shame that she is unable to maintain permanent employment.

She is a very attractive and personable lady but continually goes for the same sort of jobs that only show up her weaknesses rather than one that will play to her strengths and talents. She gets very tearful and feels hopeless when considering her future.

She has now been introduced to self-soothing coping strategies to improve her mood and emotional state and is beginning to feel calmer. She can also see that she needs to break the vicious circle where her emotions set her up for failure. She is working on improving her relationships as she is aware that she gets very defensive about any sort of criticism from work colleagues who actually have the ability to help and support her.

Observe people at work who you consider to have strong skills in emotion-based problem solving:

- Who do you know at work that looks and sounds confident in problem-solving situations involving people? Note at least two names of people who match this description.

- How do they sound? What words do they use when problem solving?

- What do you notice about the questions they ask? How do they carry themselves in meetings? How do they interact with others?

- Which aspects of how they are would you like to demonstrate more in yourself?

Use these questions to observe yourself:

- When you think about your strengths and weaknesses in problem solving based on emotion, how would you describe yourself?

- For what qualities do others seek you out?

- When you try to solve problems of an emotional nature, do you use a structured approach?

- How effective are you at solving problems of an emotion-based nature?

Distinguishing core emotions

The challenge in this skill is that we need to be able to distinguish a core emotion from other emotions. There really are only a few core emotions and these are listed below. Many other emotions or feelings are descriptive of states (see examples at the end of this section).

This specificity underpins the ability to use emotion as data. If we are able to clearly name the emotion that we are dealing with, it is much easier to be able to problem solve a situation.

See the chart below of each core emotion and what we might do to embrace it and work with it.

Emotion	What to do when you are feeling this way
Sadness *Associated with feelings of loss*	Stay with your sadness; try to understand where it has come from. Let others know you are feeling sad and that you may be quieter than usual.
Anger *Associated with feelings of being stopped by someone or something reaching our own goals*	Try to distinguish whether it is mild irritation or anger and try to grade your anger on a scale of 0 to 10. Express that you feel angry in a healthy way, and move on. (See the tips in Chapter 9 Expressing.)

Remember that anger and rage are often a cover up for feelings of loneliness, heartbreak, grief, sadness, sorrow or helplessness over others. This may be where you need to focus to achieve longer-term relief of any underlying anger. |
| **Fear** *Associated with feelings of being unable to control the outcome* | Acknowledge that you are feeling fearful (to yourself) and that this is either natural, given the situation, or unnatural, if you are imagining the worst outcome.

Take an action to self-soothe (see the tools in this chapter) and try to talk yourself out of it by remembering what is the worst thing that can happen and being accepting of that. |
| **Guilt** *Associated with feelings of violating our own values* | Write down what you feel guilty about. Write down two scores – how bad the thing is that you have done and how guilty you feel about it. Decide what you are going to do about it and then actually take action. If it is something not within your power to change, then note that this is a natural reaction and that you cannot change it now. To achieve acceptance, forgive yourself or the person who hurt you. |

Emotion	What to do when you are feeling this way
Shame *Associated with feelings of inadequacy or unworthiness through regret or remorse for something you did, whether real or imagined*	Listen to your inner voice and offer yourself caring and compassion. Use the self-soothing tools. If you are feeling shameful because an old shame has arisen from the past, this feeling should have no control over your present. If someone is doing something to make you feel ashamed, you may have to use your assertiveness to reply confidently, so that the other person can start to question the accuracy of their doubt in you.
Hopefulness *Associated with feelings of optimism*	Use the energy towards something positive.
Hopelessness *Associated with feelings of depletion and lacking talent, passion and confidence at work from making wrong decisions*	Get away from your work for a while to restore yourself. Find the activities that connect you with what you want. Use the self-soothing strategies here. Start to feel the energy of nature. Identify all the things you can do to please yourself.
Happiness/Joy *Associated with feelings of happiness*	Use the energy towards something positive.

Examples of non-core feelings

Behaviours done **to you** by someone else:

annoyed	crushed	disgusted
aggravated	defeated	disheartened
agitated	dejected	drained
alienated	demoralised	encouraged
betrayed	disappointed	enraged

exasperated	offended	stimulated
fatigued	outraged	stressed
gratified	panicked	terrified
hindered	provoked	thrilled
humiliated	shaken	used
let down	shut down	worn out
intimidated	stifled	

Mental, physical or behavioural state:

anticipatory	ecstatic	fortunate
apprehensive	elated	insecure
confused	energetic	involved
connected	energised	optimistic
depressed	engaged	overwhelmed
disengaged	enthusiastic	resigned
dissatisfied	exhausted	
distressed	exuberant	

Judgements of yourself or other people:

accomplished	determined	desperate
apathetic	lethargic	

By staying with the core feelings, it is much easier to use emotions for problem solving and to pave the way for an appropriate expression of these feelings.

Tools for problem solving

Working through the tools in this section will help you to make a longer-term shift in your emotion-based problem solving.

There are three tools included here for problem-solving emotions at work:

- **feelings check-in;**

- **self-soothing;**

- **differences and disagreements.**

1. Feelings check-in

This tool has a particular role of actually helping you to acknowledge your feelings as useful data.

Step 1. Stop what you are doing and say to yourself, 'I am feeling a feeling.' This is your call to notice that there is something important happening for you that you ignore at your peril!

Step 2. Name the feeling. Say, 'I feel... (the feeling).' Use only a core feeling in your description (sad, angry, fearful, happy/joyful, shameful, guilty).

Step 3. Remind yourself that you made yourself have this feeling to avoid the natural instinct to say things like, 'This job makes me feel this' or 'You make me feel this' and leaves the responsibility for your feelings squarely with you.

Step 4. Honour the feeling. Take care of yourself and breathe. This is to acknowledge the feeling as natural in the situation you are in.

Step 5. Work out what belief about yourself put you in the reaction. Sometimes the belief is, 'My colleague hates me'; 'I should be happy at work all the time'; 'I always get it wrong'; 'I am hopeless at this task'; 'No one cares about me. I am invisible at work.' Usually, it is a negative belief we formed from our experiences.

Step 6. Challenge the belief in order to find a solution more easily. In the examples above, our modified beliefs might be: 'My colleague made the best choice based on what they knew at the time'; 'Work is naturally full of ups and downs'; 'I try to get it right but do not always succeed and that is OK'; 'I am good at some things and am still learning other aspects of my role'; 'I can take actions to take care of myself when I need to, I do not need to rely on others for my basic self-esteem.'

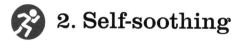 2. Self-soothing

This tool is linked with the previous two activities and offers different ways of being able to problem solve your emotions.

Self-soothing is a coping strategy, typically involving any number of the five senses (touch, taste, smell, sight and sound). Listed below are examples of self-soothing strategies for each sense that can be done at work. The idea is to engage in an activity with 100 per cent attention. Be aware of your senses and what you are experiencing. Try to do a maximum of three self-soothing activities at any one time. Be selective. It is more about quality than quantity. When you get distracted or your mind wanders, bring your attention back to the task. Come up with your own self-soothing strategies that you can do when you are upset. Try to come up with as many as you can. The more you can have in your toolkit of resources, the better off you will be in improving your mood when you are experiencing distress.

Touch

- Massage your hands, head, neck
- Get some fresh air and feel the wind/rain/sun on your face
- Stretch your arms and legs
- Change into more comfortable clothes, if possible

Taste

- Eat something soothing
- Sip herbal tea

- Eat something healthy
- Slowly suck a hard-boiled sweet

Smell

- Shop for flowers
- Smell lavender or vanilla
- Deeply breathe in fresh air

Sight

- Look at something funny (a video or a photo)
- Read something uplifting
- Look at photos of loved ones
- Look at photos of a place you like to visit
- Watch the clouds for a minute

Sound

- Listen to relaxing music
- Sing to yourself
- Say positive statements out loud to yourself for self-encouragement

3. Differences and disagreements

This tool offers different ways of perceiving the problem you face.

There are four very specific ways of approaching a difference or disagreement that you have with someone. These approaches are based on being able to neutralise emotion when it is vital for you to find a solution. Problems usually will not get resolved if you stay stuck in a feeling of anger or resentment, for example.

1. Seeing, knowing and being

This is an approach that helps you to keep an objective perspective on what is going on.

It requires you to think through:

- What do you **see** in this situation, what is your vision as a fly on the wall, if you could see what is happening very clearly and from all perspectives, not just your own?

- What do you **know** in this situation? Try to separate out what is **real** knowledge from what is **imagined** or made-up knowledge of the situation. One way of thinking about knowing is to focus on the idea that the situation is already an intelligent situation and there is some bigger meaning or purpose to what is happening right now.

- How do you need to **be** in this situation if you are not going to (1) be part of the problem through your own unhelpful behaviours and (2) avoid the wisdom from the previous two questions.

2. Self-responsibility

Every knock helps you to be strong. Suffering builds strength, if you can work out what you had responsibility for, no matter what went wrong.

So, the key question here is, 'What is the part of this situation that I am 100 per cent responsible for?' This is the part that we need to focus on, in order to find a solution.

3. Right perspective

> 'The significant problems of our time cannot be solved by the same level of thinking that created them.'
>
> ALBERT EINSTEIN, GERMAN PHYSICIST AND PHILOSOPHER OF SCIENCE

This is a very useful strategy for accepting that the person you are interacting with has the right perspective, based on their own experiences, knowledge and ideas. This can be very empowering when trying to resolve conflict. It involves shifting perspective towards acceptance of the situation rather than putting energy into the fight.

4. Flexibility

Try a more flexible approach. When you consider the problem, ask yourself:

'Is this how X would see it (where X is a person whose opinion you really value)?'

'What other ways to see this problem might there be?'

Use methods to generate ideas; consult others to generate possible solutions, no matter how crazy or silly they might seem:

'What would X advise me to do in this situation (where X is a person whose opinion you really value)?'

'What other solutions might there be?'

When you come across a colleague with a different view or approach, try to identify where your difference is – is it **values**, **beliefs** or **experiences**? This will be a helpful way of identifying how to be assertive.

When appropriate, state the differences you notice and what this means for your interaction. Where it helps, you may need to shift your own perspective from time to time.

When you hear something that you disagree with, ask yourself these three questions:

1. Does it really matter? (If yes, proceed to 2)

2. Is it to do with values or a random happening?

3. What shall I do about it? That is, what do I need to say or do to be true to my values?

Another way of experimenting with flexibility is to take a situation that feels very uncomfortable – for example, your organisation has recently bought a smaller organisation and all jobs are at risk. Write down 5 to 10 possible positive outcomes of the situation for you and focus on the different people in the scenario and what the conversations that take place might be. Whilst this is an imaginative exercise, the purpose is to force you to see a possible good outcome from an unpopular decision.

Examples:

My boss asks me to lead the change and I get a job promotion from it.

My boss' manager asks me the direct question, what would I do if I was in charge? I give her my input and she takes it on board. The advice I gave gives the team I am part of a strong position in the new structure.

The head of the smaller organisation becomes my boss and is a great leader. I learn a lot from her and, the first time I meet her, she asks me some interesting questions, which gives me an opportunity to tell her in detail what I enjoy in my work.

Chapter 9

Expressing

'Comfort in expressing your emotions will allow you to share the best of yourself with others, but not being able to control your emotions will reveal your worst.'

BRYANT H. MCGILL, AMERICAN AUTHOR

This chapter will give you:

- practical ideas for how to express yourself at work, including the value of self-disclosure;

- clear evidence that genuineness is a very important quality when you express yourself;

- a clear understanding of how to express feelings versus thoughts;

- worked examples of how to express work expectations, core feelings and appreciation;

- an insight into how to make an amend.

Expressing
Communicating your feelings and thoughts to other people at work

The definition above covers all the things we may want to express at work. The extent to which you are fluent at communicating feelings to others will affect how easy others find it to work with you. If you can express what you are feeling accurately and unambiguously to your colleagues, you will build a strong relationship with them. Many people who seem to struggle with this often have difficulty in communicating emotions.

I wonder often why we find it so difficult to let others know how we feel in the workplace. Maybe this inability to express emotion signals a problem of low self-worth? Maybe our self-control is too high and it stops us from expressing what we need to say?

The type of expression we need will vary from situation to situation. If you are trying to express your thoughts in a meeting, for example a vision to colleagues and external stakeholders, then communication that is lively, energetic, passionate and direct is likely to be more compelling and interesting for your listeners.

Where it is a question of values and hot buttons, then it may be appropriate to stand up for your own rights and beliefs and be reasonably assertive in your style of communication.

At other times, it might be more appropriate to back off, even though you know you are right.

Generally, when expressing, the use of non-verbal communication will intensify the experience of expressing emotion, including tone of voice, posture, facial expressions and gestures. It can also be useful to become aware of how you express negative emotions, for example, fear and anger.

Taken to the extreme, too much expression can lead you to being considered to be highly emotional, if you have a tendency to express emotions openly when others are more reserved or uncomfortable with this level of candidness.

On the other hand, if you do not express yourself at work, you may not be heard. If you are reluctant to disagree with people and offer feedback, you are unlikely to make progress at work.

Practical observations

1. In the workplace we do not sufficiently value people who express feelings, though people who can express their feelings usually are giving voice in a larger group.

2. Giving praise and compliments in the workplace is sorely lacking.

3. Everyone at work can practise the expression of positive feelings of happiness, amusement and joy in everyday situations.

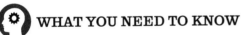 **WHAT YOU NEED TO KNOW**

1. 'Expressed emotion' has been researched extensively within psychiatric disorders by either interviewing the family members of a psychiatric patient and listening to them talk for five minutes about the patient, or asking the family member to complete a survey. These measures are designed to assess what type of emotional atmosphere

▶

is present around the patient and what is the effect of this on their probability of relapse. The expressions of emotion are quantified in categories, including critical comments, hostility and emotional over-involvement (including talking more and listening less). The researchers also note the number of positive remarks (regard) and warmth. The majority of studies have demonstrated that a significantly higher number of patients living with schizophrenia, alcohol problems and learning difficulties experience relapse when they have high expressed emotion relatives compared to patients living with low expressed emotion relatives.

2. A brain imaging study by psychologist Matthew Lieberman and colleagues at the University of California revealed the positive impact of labelling feelings with words. They studied the activity in the part of the brain known for handling strong emotional reactions like fear and panic, the amygdala. When a person was shown a photo that made them feel angry, the activity in the amygdala reduced when the label 'angry' was attached to the feeling. They described it as similar to hitting the brakes when you are driving, to slow a car down. Labelling feelings has the same effect: it slows down the brain activity in the emotions centre of the brain and this gives some credence to the value of talking about feelings.

3. Priyanka Carr and Greg Walton (2014) are two researchers at Stanford University who carried out an interesting study on groups of people with a problem to solve. One group was told they would be working on the task with other people 'together' and they would receive tips from a team member, when they were working alone in another room. The other group was told they would be working alone and would receive tips,

but from the researchers, with no mention of the word 'together'. In fact, all participants of both groups worked alone, the only difference being that one group was told they would be working 'together' with other colleagues. The effects of this small difference were significant. Participants in the group who were told they would work 'together' worked 48 per cent longer, solved more problems correctly, and had better recall for what they had seen. They also said that they felt less tired and depleted by the task. They also reported finding the puzzle more interesting when working together, and persisted longer because of this intrinsic motivation (rather than out of a sense of obligation to the team, which would be an extrinsic motivation). The word 'together' signalled to team members that they belonged, that they were connected and that there were people around them that they could trust, working with them towards the same goal. This gives a whole new meaning to paying attention to how we express words about collaboration to help people to perform at their best. It is remarkable that it does not take much effort and change to create a feeling of togetherness. Subtle cues that signal to others that they are part of a team or larger effort spark motivation and effort. Careful attention to the social context as people work and learn can help us unlock motivation.

MEET SANCHEZ

Sanchez was employed in a new role. The first few months went really well but then more personnel were recruited and gradually tensions started to arise as different people and personalities jockeyed for more power within the company. Sanchez had presumed his position was safe until the two main directors argued and one of them walked out.

Suddenly, Sanchez felt very vulnerable amongst colleagues who were not including him in discussions. They seemed to have an unnecessary resentment against him, as he had been the first one employed and they had had no input in him joining the company.

Sanchez did have one colleague whom he thought he could trust and had, what he believed, was a private conversation with him, only to find afterwards that it had been repeated to the rest of the staff. Another colleague was particularly awkward and unpleasant, making Sanchez's life as difficult as possible and expecting him to work very long hours.

No one was communicating with Sanchez now, the thought of going to work was making him ill and, eventually, he felt compelled to resign. His omission of expressing himself to his colleagues had a detrimental effect, and holding in his reactions actually cost him his well-being and his job. This could, perhaps, have been avoided through expressing how he was feeling without attributing blame to others.

Unfortunately, I met Sanchez long after this event in his life and he recognised that coaching for this situation would have been helpful: learning to express his feelings, being able to say 'no' to unnecessary demands, and help in creating a dialogue with colleagues to openly discuss what was required and expected on both sides.

Sanchez was not able to do this and, consequently, his health and self-confidence suffered for some considerable time.

 Observe people at work who you consider to have strong skills in expressing:

- Who do you know who finds it easy to express their feelings in words? What do they say, typically?

- Who do you know who finds it easy to express their feelings in actions? What do they do, typically?

- Who do you know who expresses warmth easily?

- Who do you know who can comfortably express to you how much they enjoy working with you?

- Which feelings words do they use?

- How do they deal with conflict? Is their interaction still positive, even when they experience conflict or when things do not go to plan?

- How do they stand up for their rights? What do you hear them saying?
- Do you hear them say 'no' to other people? How do they turn people down?
- Which of the observed behaviours would you like to use yourself more often?

Use these questions to observe yourself:

- In what ways do you express your feelings? Words/actions/neither way?
- To whom at work could you express how you feel, at the present time?
- When you are expressing yourself, what precedes the desire to do so?
- When you are more reserved or quiet, or allow others to dominate the conversation, what are the triggers for this?
- Are they always the same people, situations, reasons?
- How do you stand or hold your body when you are expressing yourself compared to when you are not? (For example, hunch over, avoid eye contact, and fiddle with your pen.)

Self-disclosure and vulnerability

A powerful way to express ourselves is through self-disclosure, revealing something personal about ourselves and taking a risk to show vulnerability in some way. This can be a very powerful use of communication to share your personal strengths, weaknesses, limitations at work and personal beliefs and feelings.

This helps to build understanding and trust and creates a more open and collaborative work environment with team members.

A few years ago I was introduced to the work of research professor and author Dr Brené Brown (2010, 2012, 2013). Before you go any further, watch her two videos to hear about shame, resilience and vulnerability.

 The video links are provided in the web resources.

Tools for expressing

Working through the tools in this section will help you to make a longer-term shift in your expressing.

There are five tools included here for increasing your skills in expressing yourself at work:

- **expressing feelings versus thoughts**

- **expressing expectations**

- **expressing core feelings**

- **expressing appreciation**

- **making an amendment.**

Expressing feelings versus thoughts

It is useful to realise that thinking is not the same as feeling. It is helpful to know the difference between your expression of thoughts and feelings.

Thoughts: these do not help us to describe a feeling. These undermine the impact of our message about feelings.

I feel like...

I feel that X is...

I feel like you do not...

Be aware that, when feelings are not expressed, they transition into other emotions:

- Anger becomes depression

- Fear becomes avoidance

- Guilt becomes shame

- Sadness becomes illness

- Loneliness becomes aloneness

- Boredom becomes restlessness

- Inadequacy becomes low self-worth

Examples of statements that are not feelings:

- I feel like you do not listen

- I feel like a cog in a machine

- I feel like an idiot

- I feel that it is impossible

- I feel like you do not respect me

It can be very useful to learn and use a formula for expressing emotions.

To express your negative reaction to someone's actions, requiring a simple statement of emotion:

> **Example**: 'When you do XYZ (state action), I feel ABC (state feeling).'

> **Example**: 'When you consistently do not do what you say, I feel angry.'

To express your negative experience, requiring an immediate action:

> The **situation** is... (clear description of fact).

> I am **feeling**... (make sure this is a three-word statement of feeling, for example, 'I feel angry').

> The **consequence** of the situation is... (the negative result of this situation for you, or others).

> My **request/suggestion** is... (small, specific and practical steps for the other person to do).

> **Example**: 'The situation is that we are two days late for delivering this report. I'm feeling angry and upset. The consequence is that our customer is unhappy and has lost faith in our ability to deliver. My request is that we make this a priority now for the next three hours and get this report done and sent to the customer.'

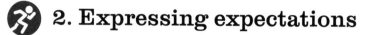

2. Expressing expectations

This tool can be used either in a new team or an existing team. You can use it with your boss or a close colleague to set very clear expectations for how you plan to work.

The two key questions are:

- What do you provide for others that they can expect from you?

- What do you expect of others that they can provide for you?

This is, ideally, a two-way conversation once you have written down your expectations as a wish list. Ideally, you talk about it and then agree the everyday mechanisms for working together.

You may wish to review the example below of a set of written expectations between two colleagues. Write your own or edit the one below with your additions and adjustments. This is a useful way of pre-empting problems in working relationships and creating a strong pattern of collaborative teamwork.

What you can expect from me/what I am providing for others:

- I will provide focused views, comments and feedback, as appropriate.

- I am fully on side with the work objectives that we set.

- I will be on time and will have respect for your time when we arrange meetings.

- When a meeting is cancelled at short notice, I will reschedule in the earliest possible time frame.

- You can expect me to be a resource for you and to share skills, knowledge and expertise within this team, as appropriate.

- I will encourage challenge and support others in all organisational activities.

What I expect of you, my colleague/what I expect us to provide together:

- We agree clear goals and deliverables together regularly.

- We are both on time and fully prepared for our meetings.

- You can accept and willingly work with any views, comments or feedback received and be open to trying new methods and approaches.

- You feel totally comfortable speaking to me when you need to.

- Whilst it is not always possible to be available in person, I expect us to both be available and contribute to in-person discussions when the topics being discussed impact all of us.

- While there is a lot that I will do to stay on track with our work goals, we have joint responsibility for making things happen and need each other to do our best work.

- We review our working relationship regularly and you alert me to any changes that would be beneficial. I am open to your feedback.

- We make a positive contribution to the organisation, the team and our customers.

3. Expressing core feelings

> 'Be who you are and say what you feel, because those who mind don't matter and those who matter don't mind.'
>
> **THEODOR SEUSS GEISEL (DR SEUSS) AMERICAN WRITER, POET AND CARTOONIST**

To get into the habit of expressing feelings, one very useful way I have found is to use a list of core feelings and to have each person in the team speak for five minutes to go through the feelings list and talk about a recent situation when they felt the feeling in the list. This quickly helps to build a much closer working relationship. The idea is to be specific rather than describe moods or accumulated emotions.

The feelings are:

- joy/happiness;

- fear;

- anger;

- sadness;

- guilt;

- shame;

- any other feeling (AOF).

- Learn to recognise when others are making unreasonable demands of you and say 'no' when you have to.

- Create scripts for yourself to follow in order to practise expressing yourself assertively.

- Choose your battles. Decide in advance what your position is, how you will express it and how far you will go with it.

- Develop alternate ways of expressing your feelings, beliefs and thoughts. If you are, typically, a person who expresses verbally, use written communication as another means.

- Communicate what you think, what you feel and what you want or need.

- Take a specific situation and ask someone you trust for advice on the assertive way to handle the situation.

- Use powerful, not powerless, language to express yourself.

- Stand up when you speak on the phone.

- If the other person does not hear you, then make a statement using the when/I/you formula – **When** you ignore me, **I** feel angry and my request is for **you** to hear me.

🏃 4. Expressing appreciation

I mentioned earlier that expressing appreciation is not a skill that is exercised often at work. An important aspect of being good at relationships is to express how you are really feeling about these relationships.

To practise this, choose three people or groups who are an important link to you in your job (for example, a key senior manager, collaborator, team member, a mentor, someone who works for you, a supplier, etc).

Considering the relationships that are working well, identify two or three specific things you really appreciate about each person and plan to express these to them using the following structure:

- State the **goal** of your communication: 'I wanted to tell you something that I don't think I have ever expressed before...'

- State the **reality** of the current situation: 'We have now been working with each other for x months/years.'

- State your **appreciation**: 'I appreciate this particular aspect of you (name the aspect).'

- State your **feeling** (using core feeling words): 'I feel very happy in our work together.'

- State the **impact** of the feeling: 'You make a positive difference in my everyday role. Thank you.'

5. Making an amend

This tool relates to situations where you have regret about the way the relationship has progressed.

Review all of your key relationships. Identify one or two relationships where there is an old hurt that you want to express. Express this to the person using the following structure:

- State the **goal** of your communication: 'I wanted to tell you something that I don't think I have ever expressed before...'

- State the **reality** of the current situation: 'We have now known each other for x years and for the last six months we have had much less contact.'

- State your **feeling** (using feeling words): 'I feel very awkward in our relationship together.'

- State a **request**: 'I wanted to ask if you could forgive me for ignoring you these last six months.'

- State the **impact** of the request: 'This will enable us to pick up where we left off and have a good relationship again. I have missed you.'

Chapter **10**

Group empathy

'Feelings are much like waves; we can't stop them from coming but we can choose which one to surf.'

JONATAN MÅRTENSSON, SWEDISH ACTOR

This chapter will give you:

- practical ideas for how to manage emotions in group situations at work;

- clear evidence that group emotion matters and can be measured;

- an understanding of how automatic assumptions can affect how you interact in teams;

- worked examples of how to understand strong emotions in a team, including how to read anger effectively;

- a simple process for checking the feelings in a team during a meeting.

Group empathy

Tuning into and shifting emotions at group level to stay on track with your work goals

A reference in *Fast Company* (a business news magazine in the USA) is the only direct mention of the term 'group empathy' that I have come across. For me, this term encompasses the skill to hold all the different perspectives in the team and to apply the three essentials we looked at earlier – empathy, understanding and caring – but with the skill to do this at a group level.

This includes taking actions, for example, to help the group shift the mood to a more positive outlook where members feel they can move forward.

Group empathy is your skill in understanding and working with other people's emotional states. People at work who are good at exercising this skill are able to influence other people's emotional states in team settings (for example, calm them down, console them and motivate them). They know how to make others feel better when they need it.

This is an essential skill for anyone in a management role, as this can help to motivate, direct and help others to develop. It is also about reaching common ground and favourable outcomes.

People who struggle with this skill become overwhelmed when they have to deal with other people's emotional outbursts and are less likely to enjoy socialising and networking.

Too much group empathy can also be counterproductive. You might be seen to be overly controlling of others' behaviour and manipulative at worst.

Today's work environments require increasingly strong teams. Our individualistic natures are no longer going to give us success without being able to work with and through other people.

Coming back to my theme of human upgrade from the introduction, coping with the level of complexity in today's workplace using the same mental equipment that was designed for a much simpler world creates significant stress. Failure to grasp the nuances of the group mind has real consequences for your effectiveness at work and your personal resilience. Group empathy is critical for effective teamwork and for getting a whole organisation behind a new idea.

Group empathy involves becoming a student of human nature in all its complexity in team situations. This requires our full set of emotional resilience tools and skills – the essentials of self-worth, self-control, mood, empathy, understanding, caring, plus the skills of problem solving, shifting, expressing and dialogue. Developing this skill at work will take practice. Ideally, all team members will be able to utilise this skill in order to be productive.

Practical observations

1. I have met few people (fewer than five) who are not counsellors that are genuinely good at this.

2. Colleagues in my field who have trained in counselling or psychotherapy with compulsory group work (group sessions, with no agenda), are usually skilled at this.

3. Leaders who read their teams well often achieve positive business results more easily.

⚙ WHAT YOU NEED TO KNOW

I think that it is really important for us to go beyond the brain and realise that we have a whole body response to our emotions, which affects our health and well-being either positively, in the case of positive emotions, or negatively, in the case of disruptive emotions like fear and anger. This matters for how we work in teams.

1. A key finding from research on the relationship between individual team members' emotional intelligence and team performance is that regulating emotions (managing emotions in oneself and in others) is of greater importance in team environments than is the ability to read and understand emotions (Rice, 1999).

2. In a study on physical touch conducted by the HeartMath Institute researchers found that, when people touch or are in proximity, one person's heartbeat signal is registered in the other person's brainwaves. This explains how sometimes we can sense the energy of the people in a meeting. Where there is friction and tension, this also registers on each other.

3. Neurocardiologist John Andrew Armour, Dalhousie University, Halifax, Nova Scotia, has discovered that the heart has its own brain and nervous systems (just like the brain). In 1991 research started to focus attention on the heart as a powerhouse of energy and intelligence. This 'heart brain' has highly sophisticated computational abilities and affects both heart and brain function. No longer can we think that our intelligence resides solely in our brain. It has been learnt that chemicals in the heart affect brain processing and virtually every other organ in the body.

4. Emotions exist as chemical reactions; studies into the molecular makeup of emotions has confirmed that emotions have a chemical signature (Pert, 1997).

5. Whole body representation of emotions involves a number of different organs and systems in the body, including the heart, brain, autonomic nervous system, hormonal system and sensory organs and, therefore, all of these influence thoughts and behaviour.

 ## MEET RICK

On paper Rick was a very successful executive in a fast-moving environment. However, he was advised to seek some coaching with me after his boss was alerted to attend some of his team meetings.

Rick is loud, boisterous and outgoing with a stream of imaginative ideas and questions but does not actually allow anyone to get a word in edgeways. He is always the centre of attention, sometimes a buffoon but always funny and his meetings are very lively. However, quieter and less confident members of the team felt they just were not loud enough to even get noticed, let alone listened to.

Rick needed to tone down his approach and bring everyone into the discussion, allowing all to be heard. Everyone has different talents and a different way of expressing themselves and Rick needed to allow for this and create a mutual atmosphere of trust.

Following coaching in which he explored this approach, he met with everyone individually and allowed them to give feedback whilst he listened – very new for Rick. Then he looked at building trust and support within the team, so everyone felt valued and that they had a contribution to make and could speak out without feeling uncomfortable.

In the next big project meeting he asked for everyone to give their ideas in a much calmer and less frenetic atmosphere where he did not dominate the meeting. Tony, the quietest team member you will ever come across, finally had the courage to speak up and had some of the most creative design ideas of all, which were immediately snapped up.

 Observe people at work who you consider to have strong skills in group empathy:

- Who do you know that is good at understanding the emotions of others in groups? Note here the names of at least two people and observe what they do.
- What do you like about how these people interact with others?
- What do they actually do? Give examples.
- How do they deal with conflict?
- Which of the observed behaviours would you like to use more often yourself?

Use these questions to observe yourself:

- What are the early warning signals for you that something is not quite right in an interaction?
- When do you most need to manage others' emotions?
- Is it the same in all groups you are part of at work?
- Are you more able to understand and work with the emotions of some people in groups more easily than others?
- Are they always the same people, situations, reasons – are some more difficult?

Tools for group empathy

Working through the tools in this section will help you to make a longer-term shift in your skills in group empathy.

1. Automatic assumptions

'The only part of us that is 100 per cent honest is our emotions.'

ANONYMOUS

This tool is focused on helping you to identify what might be going on when someone else has strong emotions in a situation.

The list below indicates the key automatic assumptions that we make when we experience negative emotion. Different assumptions are associated with the experience of different emotions. Only some of these will apply at any one time. Use the characteristics below to reflect on a situation you have experienced recently that brought up strong emotions for you.

Whenever a situation has the three characteristics below, we are likely to be working from automatic assumptions and these are situations where we need to be the most careful in our responses in teams.

For this tool to be helpful, the situation you choose needs to be relevant to your goals, something that threatens the achievement of your goals and involves something important to you being impacted negatively.

1. **The situation is relevant to your goals.** Goals can be formal goals or objectives that you set yourself, or can be informal, unstated desires like wanting to work in a productive team when your team is dysfunctional. If the situation is not relevant to your goals or to the goals of people who are important to you, then you feel little emotion. The intensity of the emotion you feel reflects the importance of the goal.

2. **The situation threatens your goals.** Usually you experience positive emotions in situations that support your achievement of goals and negative emotion when these are being frustrated. When you feel threatened, usually you have an expectation that things will turn out badly.

3. **Negative impact on you.** You experience different emotions, depending on which of the following personal factors you think are threatened. For example:

   - your self-worth or the value that other people see in you;
   - your ideal of how you want to see yourself;
   - your moral values;
   - thoughts, ideas, philosophies and understandings of reality that you consider important;
   - people that you appreciate or objects you value;

- goals and ambitions important to you;
- that you are responsible, or that someone else is to blame;
- that you have some power to affect the situation, or that you are powerless.

In these situations, we need to be very careful that our automatic assumptions do not get the better of us.

2. Emotion analysis

This is a useful approach for understanding your own strong emotions, as well as those of others. It helps us to see whether the emotions we are experiencing are alerting us to something important or just an over-reaction to the circumstances.

Follow these steps:

Step 1. Relax! Once you recognise the emotion, you need to let it pass so you can think clearly and objectively. If you are able to, use relaxation techniques to calm down.

Step 2. Identify the assumptions you are making. Start by using points in the previous activity. Use these as a checklist, but also identify any other assumptions that are influencing the emotion.

Step 3. Challenge the assumptions. Approaching each one by one, challenge it rationally to see whether the assumption is correct or not. The table below shows examples of some of the emotions that you might experience, the assumptions that lie behind them, and the challenges that you might make to these assumptions.

- With each challenge, identify whether the assumptions you have made are correct or incorrect. Be fair.
- Take action appropriately. Where your assumptions are incorrect, the negative emotions should change or disappear as soon as you acknowledge this.
- Where assumptions either have some element of truth to them or are fully correct, then you need to recognise this. Think through what you need to do to manage these situations. This may include drawing on skills explained elsewhere in this book.

- Where you are sure of the foundation of the negative emotion, then you have the option to use it for good effect. In the right circumstances, feeling angry can provide tremendous power and motivation but may damage relationships.

- The table below gives you some prompt questions that can be used in a group when you detect a core feeling. These questions can help to change the mood, progress with a meeting, and open up essential dialogue.

Assumptions underlying negative emotions

Emotion	Description	Underlying assumption	Points to check
Anger	A strong feeling of annoyance, displeasure or hostility when one is attacked, insulted, deceived or frustrated.	Frustration of important goals. Damage to self-worth, or to people, objects or ideas you value. Blamed on another person or group of people.	What goals are being challenged? Are they appropriately important? Are they really being frustrated, or is there a way around this? How severe is the damage? Is blame fairly attributed and shared?
Anxiety	A feeling of worry, nervousness or unease about something with an uncertain outcome.	Thoughts that others are judging you badly. Preoccupation with self, so can't focus on other aspects of experience and don't hear what others are saying. Sense of not belonging. Interpret events in terms of perceived threat to you.	Is the anxiety real and serious? How likely are the imagined outcomes to occur? Is there appropriate action can take to mitigate the risk? What are the realistic consequences of the situation? Are there steps you can take to recover the situation?

Emotion	Description	Underlying assumption	Points to check
Fear	An unpleasant emotion caused by the threat of physical or emotional danger, pain or harm.	Threat to your survival or what you hold to be important. Uncertainty about whether the threatened situation will occur or its severity. No internal or external blame.	Is the threat real and serious? What are the realistic consequences of the situation? Are there steps you can take to recover the situation?
Guilt	The feeling when you realise or believe that you caused moral harm or violated a moral standard.	Threat to your survival or what you hold to be important. Internal conflict. Feeling that doesn't go away easily.	Did the event really occur as you describe it to yourself? Is this a moral standard that you should respect, or is it one that is inconsistent with your viewpoint on reality? Is there an objective reason that it is as important as you think it is? How completely did you fail to live up to it? Are you setting yourself unreasonable targets? Are you completely to blame for the situation, or is someone else fully or partly responsible? Are there steps you can take to recover the situation or make an amendment?

Emotion	Description	Underlying assumption	Points to check
Shame	A feeling of distress caused by awareness of wrong behaviour or not living up to ideal standards.	Failure to live up to an important moral standard. Blame on yourself.	Did the event really occur as you describe it to yourself? Is this an ideal that is reasonable and achievable? Is there an objective reason that it is as important as you think it is? How completely did you fail to live up to the ideal? Are you setting yourself unreasonable targets? Are you completely to blame for the situation, or is someone else partly or fully responsible? Are there steps you can take to recover the situation?
Sadness	Emotional pain associated with feelings of loss, disadvantage, despair, hopelessness or sorrow.	Failure to live up to an expectation of life or relationship. Blamed on ourselves.	Is the damage real? How serious is it? Is there really no ability to recover the situation, or is there something that can be done about it?

Source: Descriptions of emotions based on Lazarus, R.S. (1993) 'Why We Should Think of Stress as a Subset of Emotion', *Handbook of Stress* (Eds Golderberger, L. and Breznitz, S.). New York: The Free Press.

3. Managing anger in group situations

Anger in groups is a feeling that many people find difficult to deal with. This tool provides a structure to understand why others might be becoming angry in a team situation.

If you suspect that someone is angry, it is worth asking yourself three questions:

1. Is the prevention of achieving a goal by someone or something *important* to you or another team member?

2. Is this potentially damaging to your own or someone else's self-esteem, hurting people in the group or contrary to the ideas the group considers important?

3. Does someone think that you or another individual is responsible for this situation?

If you answer yes to all three questions, this situation requires you to have the ability to read anger effectively.

Here are some practical tips for managing anger:

- Recognise and understand the level of your own emotions as well as the emotions of the people you are interacting with: really angry, or just over-excited? Are you slightly worried, or profoundly fearful?

- Determine the source of the feelings. Is it really a bad experience in the past, rather than something that is occurring now?

- Talk about feelings – yours and the other person's. Acknowledge them and deal with them directly. Express your own feelings in a non-confrontational way. This can be done, for example, by using I-messages, where you say, 'I feel angry because...' rather than, 'You made me angry by...' The first approach explains your feelings without accusing anyone else, while the second focuses blame on the other person who is likely to become hostile or defensive in response.

- Acknowledge the other persons' feelings as legitimate. Although you may feel differently about a situation, the other person's feelings are real and denying their existence or validity is just likely to intensify those feelings.

- Do not react emotionally to emotional outbursts.

- If you are having trouble staying calm, temporarily leave the room. By leaving the scene, you have a chance to calm down and think. You can then plan an effective response, rather than reacting automatically, which often makes the situation worse.

- Use symbolic gestures. Gestures such as apologies, sympathy notes, shared meals, or even handshakes can be very useful in expressing respect and defusing negative emotions at little cost.

4. Team check-in

In a team meeting, you might find that there are emotions below the surface that have not yet been expressed. A simple tool to use in situations like this, involves pausing and asking everyone to think for a moment and then to share two statements: what they are **thinking** about the topic; and what they are **feeling** about the topic.

Often these two items will give completely different inputs.

Use this structure to understand why others are feeling stuck or why the meeting is not progressing:

1. Pause for a few minutes so that everyone can collect their thoughts before they speak.

2. Go around the room and ask everyone to summarise in two sentences their perspective on the topic/meeting/discussion:

   - **Thinking** – 'What are you thinking about this topic?'
   - **Feeling** – 'What are you feeling about this topic?'

3. There should be no discussion; each person speaks for 30 seconds to 1 minute maximum and everyone else listens to their input.

4. Once everyone has spoken, ask the team. 'Given what we have just heard, what is the best way to spend the remaining time in our meeting?'

Chapter 11

Dialogue

'The intimacy of work is like the intimacy of marriage.
Both involve vows.'

DAVID WHYTE, ENGLISH POET

This chapter will give you:

- practical ideas for how to engage open and honest dialogue in team situations at work;

- evidence of the physiology of emotion that can be generated in dialogue;

- tools for engaging dialogue on both practical topics and more difficult conversations, including how to give feedback;

- a summary of emotions that stops us from challenging others and building trusting relationships.

Dialogue
Discussing feelings when there is a problem

Earlier we focused on the essentials of empathy, understanding and caring, which create a strong basis for connection. Dialogue skills are about both being able to handle difficult moments effectively and being proactive about what types of conversation to initiate within a team.

The reality is that, through talking, you can change the group dynamics. In the absence of conversation, there is often a gap in performance or effectiveness. Having effective dialogue involves not only the skill of reflecting and absorbing but also taking an active role.

Without dialogue, it is likely that there is guesswork involved in trying to read other people. When done well, dialogue helps to break through difficult situations.

Often our fear stops us, so this chapter is about building the skill of knowing when to have dialogue and how to engage it.

Practical observations

1. Many line managers shirk the responsibility of giving feedback to a colleague, even when they can see problems and when they are suffering as a result of the lack of performance or efficiency of an individual.

2. In most teams there is a total absence of dialogue about **how** the team is working (its operating methods, its way of doing its work, how people are feeling in the team) and, typically, there is a more usual focus on **what** the team is doing.

3. Discussing feelings is typically not valued and the complication is that all experiences involve information from feelings, so vital perspectives are lost to a team.

 WHAT YOU NEED TO KNOW

1. Neuropsychologist Rick Hanson (2009) and colleagues have studied how people manage their emotions at work and which emotions evolve in workplace situations. He asked people to consider 28 hypothetical workplace scenarios. He found that the following emotions were the most frequently experienced at work: frustration, anxiety, fear, irritation and depression.

2. He also found that for 60 per cent of the sample of people studied, the following 6 work situations had evoked strong emotions:

   • the tension between managing work and home life;

   • work overload – an unrealistic balance between work tasks and time to complete them;

   • company support – from 'well supported' to 'left out in the cold';

   • promotion – from 'very positive emotions' to apathetic, for example, 'about time too';

   • underskilled – feeling overwhelmed with new skill demands (often people skills);

   • delegation – sharing work tasks with others who often have different needs, agendas, priorities and speeds of work.

3. In a study by the Mayo Clinic in Minnesota, the ▶

medical histories of 839 people were tracked over 30 years – they had all completed a standard personality test between 1962 and 1965 measuring their optimism (124 optimists, 197 pessimists and 518 in between). Their death rates were compared and every 10-point increase in pessimism was associated with a 19 per cent increase in death rate. Staying optimistic means that we are likely to live longer.

4. Gender differences: in a recent study at the Indiana University School of Medicine, 10 men and women were studied while they listened to a John Grisham thriller. MRI scans (which measure high-speed changes in neural blood flow) were used to compare activity in their brains. Researchers found that women use their whole brain whereas men use half of their brain.

5. Positive emotion influences our perception of time. Kimberley Babb of the University of California presented a study at the American Psychological Society in December 2000 on the effect of emotions on our perception of time. She used film clips to induce one of 4 emotional states in 128 students – happiness, sadness, fear and neutral – and she then set them to a task. They were asked to guess when a minute had elapsed. The students who were neutral or happy were able to guess accurately the passage of one minute, but the students who were fearful or sad overestimated the time – so our emotional state affects our perception of time.

MEET MICHAEL

Recently I was coaching a client who is a board member of a well-known company. He was working with a new chief executive and, after a few weeks, I asked Michael how many times he had given any praise to his colleague, the chief executive. His initial reaction was that he did not think this would be necessary, as surely she would know that she was doing a good job. I reminded Michael that most people do not receive praise at work for what they do well. He made a mental note to give her more praise.

Over a period of weeks, I heard that he had started to offer praise, but the complaint I heard from the CEO was that the praise did not come across as being genuine. In other words, Michael was using the right words and saying the right things, but not in a way that came across as sincere.

So, it was important for Michael to focus not only on what he was saying and what he thought about his colleague but also on the feelings themselves, so that he could start to convey what it felt like to work with his new colleague. This took a few different attempts to get at the source of the problem. It required him to create more dialogue in his working relationships, which was a new habit for him.

In their own way, both Michael and the chief executive started to express what was important for them. The chief executive started to express healthy boundaries by outlining what she needed and what the consequence would be if the work was not delivered by her colleague. Michael started to offer praise but more in terms of feelings language. The combined joint effort between them made a positive impact on their working relationship.

MEET MARTINE

When I met Martine she felt she was being ostracised by her team mates and there was a very uncomfortable atmosphere in the office.

Following discussions with her colleagues, it transpired that they thought Martine was slacking in her work responsibilities and leaving them to do too much. Whilst they had their heads down working, she took frequent breaks and, if her work was not completed on time and she had to work late, she would expect time in lieu to cover this. Gradually, this caused tension and animosity amongst the team.

The team manager was reluctant to give any feedback, as this would be a difficult conversation. However, unless the situation was addressed, the office environment was going to get progressively worse.

Dialogue really should have taken place much sooner than it did for all concerned. Martine was taking breaks because she felt insecure in her skills and really needed additional training, but was embarrassed to ask. Her lack of self-confidence in this area exacerbated her smoking habit (she was the only smoker in the office), so she needed to take more breaks for that, too.

In addition, she was sociable and wanted to meet with other departments to get a broader view of what was happening within the company. In contrast, the rest of the team, although hardworking, kept more to their desks and did not mingle, and so were regarded by other departments as aloof.

So, consequently, Martine was offered more training to support her, and the rest of team was told to get out more!

 Observe people at work who you consider to have strong skills in dialogue:

- Who do you know that is good at engaging in dialogue with others? Note here the names of at least two people and try to observe what they do.

- How do they draw out people's views and perspectives?

- What do you like about how these people have dialogue with others?

- How do they deal with differences in opinion?

- Which of the observed behaviours would you like to use yourself more often?

Use these questions to observe yourself:

- What are the early warning signals for you that a working relationship needs some dialogue?

- When do you most need to have dialogue (any particular situations or topics)?

- Is it the same in all teams you are part of at work?

- Are you able to have dialogue with some people more easily than others?

- Are they always the same people, situations, topics that you find more difficult?

Hormonal system and emotions

When considering tools for dialogue, there is an important scientific finding that is relevant to understanding what we are hoping to gain for our emotional resilience through engaging dialogue. I am grateful to the HeartMath Institute for providing me with these insights when I started out in the field of emotion in 1999.

 You will find two articles in the web resources about HeartMath.

Our hormonal system is regulated partly by the brain's emotional circuits. A key daily rhythm is our daily variation in cortisol and DHEA levels. In recent years, a number of researchers have proposed the DHEA/cortisol ratio to be a good biological marker of stress and ageing. Each of these hormones is explained below.

- Cortisol is one of the most important hormones in the body, as it has a central role in metabolism, health, memory and learning, as well as in the body's ability to be immune to disease. It is released in response to stress and a low level of blood glucose. In balanced amounts, cortisol is essential for the healthy functioning of our bodies. Our cortisol level usually peaks between 07:00 am and 08:00 am and then declines to a low between 23:00 and midnight. Anyone who is under chronic stress would have high levels of cortisol. Cortisol is sometimes referred to as the stress hormone because it is secreted in excessive amounts when people are under stress.

- DHEA is the body's natural antidote to cortisol; it is known as the anti-ageing hormone and is thought to be a natural antidepressant. Its effects include enhancement of the immune system, stimulation of bone deposits, lowering cholesterol levels and building muscle mass. It can improve memory, slow down the ageing process and prevent cancer. Levels of DHEA can be increased naturally through positive emotion.

- The body is not able to produce both DHEA and cortisol at the same time, so, with high levels of cortisol, the production of DHEA often will be restricted. When individuals are under prolonged stress, cortisol levels continue to rise while DHEA levels decrease significantly – this creates an imbalance, the effects of which can be severe and may include elevated blood sugar levels, increased bone loss, compromised immune function, decreased skin repair and regeneration, increased fat accumulation and brain cell destruction. When cortisol levels rise too high, it can be extremely dangerous to us. A study reported in the September (2000) issue of *Psychosomatic Medicine* suggested that slender women who have higher levels of cortisol (the stress hormone) tend to have more abdominal fat – which is known to increase the risk of several disorders, including heart disease and diabetes.

- Being aware of this hormonal balance gives an important area on which to focus, in order to stay emotionally resilient at work. We need to find ways to increase DHEA and reduce cortisol. Natural ways to increase DHEA can be learned through the use of focused breathing techniques (see Chapter 7 Shifting). Replacing cortisol with DHEA, through activating positive emotion, can reduce cortisol levels. Feeling happy at work is actually good for your health, and this explains why some people often look younger than their years (lots of DHEA) or have aged too quickly through not wearing their stress well (high levels of cortisol).

Tools for dialogue

The tools in this chapter are focused on increasing DHEA and lowering cortisol through dealing proactively with any issues that are lingering around, but doing this in an effective way.

Working through the tools in this section will help you to make a longer-term shift in your skills in dialogue.

 ## 1. Team talk

The following list of questions is designed to engage dialogue on the emotional content of teamwork. Ask these questions of your team:

1. Have we started to talk about feelings?

2. Have we started to respect them?

3. Have we started to assign value to feelings?

4. Have we included feelings in our decision making and problem resolution?

5. Have we been prepared to change track with a decision, if it is creating negative emotion?

6. Have we listened to the most sensitive people in the team?

7. Have we struck a balance between emotion and logic?

8. Have we done our part in making our workplace somewhere that feelings are mutually respected?

9. Have we established how we wish our colleagues and customers to feel in terms of their emotional experience of doing work/business with us?

10. Have we used other activities in this book to understand and notice feelings?

When getting the team's input, it can be helpful to start by setting some ground rules or guidelines for the team talk, so that you create the conditions for having a sensible conversation. For one-on-one conversations with team members, it can be useful to make suggestions on how the meeting can be effective. If the meeting is taking place in person, you might want to display these guidelines visually in the meeting:

1. Please let go of the past.

2. Please speak the truth.

3. Please be supportive and helpful, not cynical or negative.

4. Pick something that you can improve about yourself.

🏃 2. Dialogue on hot buttons

In Chapter 7 Shifting, you were asked to identify your hot buttons, and you identified the ones that you need to discuss or acknowledge. From my experience, many problems can be resolved just by identifying the areas of difficulty ahead of any conflict arising.

The next activity provides a more structured approach for having this type of conversation.

This activity is designed to help you formulate a conversation with your colleague on areas that you find difficult. It covers seven steps to a more productive working relationship. You may want to work on each step and then discuss it; leave it to one side and then return to it after a few days. Each step involves you and your colleague giving your own view.

Usually it is not a good idea to try to do all these steps in one go. (Rome wasn't built in a day...).

Step 1. Respect, support, listening

What do the words respect, support and listening mean to each of you? What is your evidence that they exist in your working relationship?

	My meaning and evidence:	My colleague's meaning and evidence:
Respect	Examples: = letting me speak = silence in the conversation	Examples: = supporting my career = engaging in conversation
Support	Examples: = being a shoulder to cry on = asking if I am OK	Examples: = letting me decide how to do my work = saying it is OK for me to speak out in team meetings
Listening	Examples: = being able to listen openly = not interrupting	Examples: = picking the moments to talk and the moments to listen = not interrupting

Wherever you notice big differences between you, discuss what you are both willing to compromise and what you are attached to keeping.

Step 2. Trust

Discuss how you each believe trust is shown.

	I show my trust for my colleague through these actions:	My colleague demonstrates trust of me by these actions:
Trust	Examples: • Listening • Giving support, being non-judgemental • Spending time enjoying our work together	Examples: • Agreeing to participate in meetings • Working very closely on the same projects • Sharing workload

Again, pick out the areas that indicate the most difference between you and discuss them together. Many colleagues do not have this kind of conversation and it can help to avoid problems later on.

Step 3. Working relationship

On a scale of 0 to 10 where 0 means not at all and 10 means very much, to what extent do you each experience the following feelings in your working relationship? Circle a score between 0 and 10 in response to each feeling. Do your ratings first and then ask your colleague to do theirs.

	Me Scale of 0 to 10	My colleague Scale of 0 to 10
Appreciated*	0–1–2–3–4–5–6–7–8–9–10	0–1–2–3–4–5–6–7–8–9–10
Free*	0–1–2–3–4–5–6–7–8–9–10	0–1–2–3–4–5–6–7–8–9–10
Respected*	0–1–2–3–4–5–6–7–8–9–10	0–1–2–3–4–5–6–7–8–9–10
Understood*	0–1–2–3–4–5–6–7–8–9–10	0–1–2–3–4–5–6–7–8–9–10
Valued*	0–1–2–3–4–5–6–7–8–9–10	0–1–2–3–4–5–6–7–8–9–10
Judged	0–1–2–3–4–5–6–7–8–9–10	0–1–2–3–4–5–6–7–8–9–10
Controlled	0–1–2–3–4–5–6–7–8–9–10	0–1–2–3–4–5–6–7–8–9–10

On the feelings marked with an asterisk with a score below 7, discuss what would help you to feel more appreciated, free, respected, understood and valued.

On the other feelings with a score of between 3 and 6, discuss what would help you to feel less judged and controlled.

Step 4. Conflict

Decide on a method for resolving conflicts (for example, how quickly you might apologise for something that you have done that you feel bad about; changing demands to preferences; asking yourself what you can do to feel better in a situation; taking responsibility for feelings and not blaming the other person).

My ideal way of resolving conflict:	My colleague's ideal way of resolving conflict:

Step 5. Unhelpful patterns

Discuss the unhelpful ways in which you react when you do not get your way (for example, storm off, withhold affection or support, walk away, say mean things).

My unhelpful patterns:	My colleague's unhelpful patterns:

What needs to change to avoid conflict or unhelpful situations?

Step 6. Values

What is important to each of us in terms of values in how we go about our work?

Examples:

admiration	expression	logic	quality
approval	faith	love	reason
attention	fame	manners	relationships
authority	family	material wealth	religion
cleanliness	freedom	obedience	respect
communication	friendship	organisation	security
competition	happiness	others' opinions	self-sacrifice
conformity	hard work	pain avoidance	self-reliance
cooperation	health	peace	serenity
distraction	honesty	popularity	status
education	image	power	success
efficiency	independence	punishment	tradition
entertainment	integrity	quiet	truth
equality	knowledge	reality	winning

My values:	My colleague's values:

What are your key differences?

Step 7. Expectations

What do you expect from each other? This might include your expectations in terms of time, working relationship, quality of listening, etc.

Try not to mix expectations with needs. Needs are based on insecurity and dependency. If you believe you need someone, you probably believe you cannot work without him or her.

What I expect from my colleague:	What my colleague expects from me:

Once you have worked through this, it will enable you to have very clear expectations and roles in the relationship.

3. Trust your colleague

This tool helps you to focus on the qualities of trust in a working relationship.

For many years, I have pondered the word trust. Many people say, 'I just don't trust that person,' but what is it exactly that makes up trust in the workplace? We can enjoy working with colleagues but we may not be able to trust them with everything. In return they might not give up time for us when we need it. Perhaps absolute and enduring trust is a rare thing and we can be tolerant of small breaches of trust, such as a colleague not turning up at the agreed time (but not every time!). It is my view that good working relationships are based on **TRUST**, where:

T stands for truthfulness

R stands for respect

U stands for understanding

S stands for support

T stands for time

Whilst each of us may experience these qualities in different ways, when any of these are missing, the working relationship may not be productive. This activity helps you to check the state of five current relationships. This will help to identify what needs to change in each one.

STEP 1. Review

Take time to review your five most significant relationships against this acronym to see what is missing (see table overleaf):

STEP 2. Dialogue

Discuss with your colleague what you have discovered:

- the qualities that are present in the relationship;

- the qualities that need more emphasis.

So, you are at the point where you have discovered what is missing; let us now focus on the emotions that might get in the way of achieving **TRUST**. As you go through these, identify the ones that are stopping you achieving full **TRUST** in your relationships at work. Place a tick next to the ones that you experience.

Emotions that can get in the way of **T**ruthfulness:

- **Fear** – we may have been hurt before.

- **Anxiety** – will they like us if they know the whole truth about us?

- **Uncertainty** – will they want to know me if they really understood what was going on? Will they find out that I am a sham?

Emotions that can get in the way of **R**espect:

- **Fear** – will they be able to respect me?

- **Anger** – I am annoyed at what they have done to me and I just cannot forgive them.

Emotions that can get in the way of **U**nderstanding:

- **Selfishness** – believing that it is more important for others to understand me, believing that I am more important and I have more interesting things to say that stop me listening.

	Person 1	Person 2	Person 3	Person 4	Person 5
Truthfulness • Expressing emotions – how I feel – as well as facts • Being honest, even about the difficult areas of my work • Doing what I say • Avoiding excuses – telling the truth, even when it hurts • Not being afraid of saying it how it is	Yes/No	Yes/No	Yes/No	Yes/No	Yes/No
Respect • Accepting the person as they are – not wanting to change them • Listening when the other person speaks • Asking for their opinion • Maintaining confidential information • Checking understanding – not making assumptions • Accepting what the other person is • Not blaming them • Being open and non-judgemental • Not taking advantage of them – valuing them always • Asking how they would feel before making decisions that affect them	Yes/No	Yes/No	Yes/No	Yes/No	Yes/No
Understanding • Accepting their flaws • Being in tune with what they are saying • Listening intuitively for the essence of what is being said • Being able to sense when something is wrong before the	Yes/No	Yes/No	Yes/No	Yes/No	Yes/No

	Yes/No	Yes/No	Yes/No	Yes/No	Yes/No

- Providing constructive feedback
- Asking relevant questions
- Tolerating different views
- Respecting different points of views – yours and others
- Actively listening
- Being able to reiterate what someone is saying, accurately
- Being able to have a real conversation, even when there is no crisis happening

Support
- Being available to support when needed
- Making relevant offers of skills and resources
- Building up each person's confidence
- Accepting the person, warts and all
- Asking for help when you need it/giving help when it is needed
- Being an advocate for that person
- Allowing the person to share their problems without judgement
- Being there in time of need
- Understanding and contributing to each other

	Yes/No	Yes/No	Yes/No	Yes/No	Yes/No

Time
- Making time
- Spending quality time
- Being able to be silent – and give time to the other person
- Listening
- Valuing each other's time
- Giving space and time

	Yes/No	Yes/No	Yes/No	Yes/No	Yes/No

- **Fear** – will anyone understand me? People are too complex to even try to understand.

- **Anger** – everyone has been so awful to me, why should I bother?

- **Sadness** – if only I had had more understanding earlier in my life.

Emotions that can get in the way of **S**upport:

- **Fear** – what would it be like if I really felt cared for?

- **Anger** – everyone has been so awful to me, why should I bother with anyone else? I have been so hard done by.

Emotions that can get in the way of **T**ime:

- **Lack of commitment** – do I really believe in this relationship enough to make and keep promises?

4. Giving feedback

> 'The emotional health of a team depends on how well they air their grievances.'
>
> **ADAPTED FROM DANIEL GOLEMAN, AMERICAN AUTHOR, PSYCHOLOGIST AND SCIENCE JOURNALIST**

When given effectively, feedback can be useful for improving performance at work. Whether we are learning new skills or doing a routine job, feedback from others can help us to improve. Without feedback, it is likely we will not have a realistic perspective on how we are doing and areas we could change.

Many people avoid having feedback conversations, particularly difficult ones that evoke emotional responses. At work, managers often wait until the annual performance review to give feedback, blindsiding employees about events that, by then, are ancient history. Employees may hesitate to give feedback to their bosses for fear of retaliation. Research by Gallup shows that, in the workplace, giving no feedback may be more detrimental than giving mostly negative feedback. Learning how to give and receive feedback can help increase your confidence to conduct these conversations and create a culture that embraces feedback.

To be able to give honest feedback, a person needs to trust that you will listen to them, and not retaliate if you disagree with their input. To really hear and incorporate feedback, you need to trust that the person giving you feedback has your best interest at heart and that their motivation is to be helpful. If there is a high level of fear and low level of trust, feedback will either not occur or it will, potentially, damage relationships.

Talk about how and when you like to receive feedback. This establishes a positive framework for normalising feedback as an important part of the relationship.

Give as much positive feedback as you do negative. It is a lot easier to give negative feedback if you have given the person ample positive feedback in the past.

Feedback guidelines

BE SPECIFIC

When giving feedback, use behaviourally specific language. We have a tendency to be vague with our language when giving feedback. We hear feedback statements like: 'You need to be more of a team player,' or 'You did a great job.' That kind of feedback may get your general point across, but it does not convey enough information to help the person know exactly what they did or what they can do to improve. Instead of, 'You need to be more of a team player,' you might say, 'I noticed in the meeting today that you didn't invite other members of the team to contribute to the discussion. I think you might generate a better solution if you got more input from others on the team.' This feedback conveys specific information about the behaviour, so the person understands what she/he did.

BE TIMELY

The closer to the event you address the behaviour, the better. The exception to this is when the situation is highly emotional; the feedback can be delayed for a while. In that case, wait until everyone has calmed down before you engage in feedback. It is very difficult for people to hear it when they are in a high emotional state.

PREPARE YOUR COMMENTS

If possible, think about or write down some points so you are clear about what you are going to say. This helps you stay on track and stick to the issues. Do not think about it as a script, but rather a conversation guide.

DESIGN THE SPACE, PLACE AND TIME

Do you have this conversation over lunch or in your office? Is this conversation best had on a Friday afternoon before a long holiday or first thing on Monday morning? Do I sit behind a desk or reserve a conference room? Do I do this on the phone or face to face? Choose the space, place and time that will be most conducive to productive conversation.

MANAGE YOUR NON-VERBAL BEHAVIOUR

Most feedback (there are exceptions) is more effective when delivered with compassion and empathy. Those emotions are expressed mostly through voice tone and other non-verbal expressions. The person to whom you are speaking will unconsciously tune in more to your non-verbal communication than to your words.

CONSIDER THE INDIVIDUAL'S FEEDBACK STYLE

Some people want very direct feedback. Others need a little more indirect approach with a lot of validation. This is highly dependent upon your relationship with the person and her/his personality.

SEPARATE THE INTENTION FROM THE OUTCOME

When people make mistakes, usually they do not mess up on purpose. Sometimes, however, we assume they did do it on purpose. Do not get hung up on their intention. Focus on the behaviour and its impact.

FINALLY....

Prepare – get yourself into a neutral/objective mindset by using the tools of shifting (see Chapter 7).

5. Preparing and delivering feedback

Use the steps below in preparing and delivering feedback. To be effective, however, these steps should go hand in hand with the guidelines above. Remember that feedback is a conversation designed to be helpful not confrontational. If you find yourself being triggered during the conversation, you may need to use the skills of shifting in Chapter 7.

Situation: describe the situation and context in which the behaviour occurred. You may want to ask permission of the person to discuss this.

Example: 'Can I talk to you about your presentation in the team meeting yesterday?'

Behaviour: use behaviour-specific, non-judgemental language to describe the behaviour that occurred.

Example: 'I noticed that, when people asked you questions, you crossed your arms and looked away as they were talking.'

Outcome: state what happened as a result of the behaviour and use dialogue about the outcome to test for buy-in. Explore their perception and listen without judgement.

Example: 'As a result, very few people asked questions and may not have fully understood all of your data. I do not think that was your intention, but I think that was the outcome. What were your observations?'

Alternative behaviour: suggest a more effective alternative behaviour or ask them to suggest one.

Example: 'I might have looked at the person as they asked the question and thanked them for their question.'

Alternative outcome: discuss the possible outcome(s) if the alternative behaviour is enacted.

Example: 'As a result, you probably would have received more questions and people would have been better informed when they left the meeting.'

Part 3

The Results

Combining the **essentials** with the **skills**, you are in a strong position to produce four very important **results**: to have the energy to achieve; to sustain high performance under pressure; to build connection through quality relationships; and have influence at work with key stakeholders no matter how complex or political your workplace. These characteristics are very visible in the workplace and are the obvious signs of being emotionally resilient.

You will learn how to fine-tune your resilience through these four topics. Your competence in these four areas is the result of effectiveness in personal and team resilience.

Chapter 12

Energy

'People with high levels of personal mastery [...] cannot afford to choose between reason and intuition or head or heart any more than they would choose to walk with one leg or see with one eye.'

PETER SENGE, AUTHOR OF *THE FIFTH DISCIPLINE*

This chapter will give you:

- an insight into how energy is a result of the skills of emotional resilience as well as the essentials being in place;

- three tools for being able to keep track of your energy at work, including an energy audit, a values audit and SWAN, a way of logging regularly how your job is fulfilling your needs at a basic level.

Energy

Sustaining your strength and vitality to perform at your best

Energy is recognisable instantly when you have it at work. Far from being lethargic, you are able to direct yourself to the task at hand. With the essentials in place and exercising the skills highlighted, you are going to be in good shape to be emotionally resilient. But what can you do to check continually that your energy is directed in the best way?

Energy is having your motivation, your attention and your attitude all aligned. You feel motivated in your work, you are focused on what you have to do and you feel a positive drive to do things well. The feeling of having energy includes a sense that you are doing service for others and being of service to your employer (or your own company or customers). This can be a very useful source of energy beyond the income that you earn.

Energy affects our drive and need to produce high quality work. With energy we are likely to be more determined and to persevere when we hit problems. Our sense of achievement and motivation come from within. When we need a lot of encouragement to get things done, our energy is depleted and we are more likely to give up in the face of challenges if we do not have the incentives or perks to keep going.

Researchers have confirmed that decision fatigue (also known as ego depletion) affects people at work who have to make decisions all day, repetitively. This was studied initially with judges in court making parole judgements on prisoners. A total of 1,100 parole decisions were analysed to identify patterns when judges did not grant parole. The reality was that, the more choices the judges made in a day, the more worn out they were and therefore did not grant parole at certain times of day (Tierney, 2011 reporting on research by Levav of Stanford, and Danziger of Ben Hurion University). The risk of decision fatigue is that, simply, you are just not able to decide and you end up doing one of two things: becoming impulsive and often reckless in your decision, or not being able to make a decision at all. The challenge with decision fatigue is that it may not be that obvious to people around you. It may not be obvious to us when we are experiencing it ourselves. The challenge is to be aware of it, and to make decisions proactively to not allow it to affect us.

A different researcher, Baumeister, looked further into this to understand why decision fatigue happens and what to do about it (Tierney and Baumeister, 2011). He discovered that we have only a certain amount of energy for exerting self-control and willpower. When we have reached our limit of giving out mental energy, we are exhausted and lose the willpower and self-control to decide. For example, if I showed you 100 items from an office and I asked you to go through each item with me and make a choice between pairs of items (a) and (b), (a) and (c), and so on, you would end up exhausted. However, if I asked you simply to chat about your experience of each object without any need to decide anything, this would be much less demanding of your mental energy. Supermarket designers understood decision fatigue years ago. This explains why we see tempting sugary snacks close to the till in supermarkets, after we have made all our buying choices and both willpower and self-control are at a low point. We are more likely to give in to the temptation of our sugar cravings and we will not be able to walk past our favourite chocolate. A sugar hit (glucose) helps to give us temporary relief from decision fatigue and increases our self-control and willpower. Interestingly, this same relief is not obtained from sugar-free products or from synthethic sugars.

In learning about emotional resilience, this can be very useful for taking action to keep our willpower and our self-control high. For our brain to generate both the self-control and willpower we need, we rely on having glucose (ideally in the form of protein and nutritional food, rather than junk food and sweets) to function well. Rick Hanson in his book *Buddha's Brain* (2009) provides a summary of which supplements are useful in our diets.

 A brief list is available in the web resources.

Today we are overwhelmed with the number of distractions we have, even at the most simple level of deciding what to look at on our smartphones. Check email? Send texts? Read Facebook news feed? Connect with people I know on Linked In? Tweet? Download a new app I heard about? Watch news? Check Messenger? Listen to music? Take a photo? Capture something hilarious on video and send it to out to my friends? Look ahead to the weekend? You may have arrived at work on time today but, with all these distractions, you can escape from work in a flash. It is hardly surprising that the engagement figures in organisations are so low. Maybe we are dealing with chronic decision fatigue?

The good news is that we can learn to structure our lives to reduce the amount we experience decision fatigue by making sure we do not plan back-to-back commitments (we need time to breathe and rekindle our willpower and self-control), by having self-discipline to take breaks, to get good rest at night and not make a decision or have an important conversation on an empty stomach.

This chapter focuses on three essential tools you can use to keep your energy high – energy audit, values audit and SWAN. These activities will help you to be more conscious of how you are giving and replenishing your energy.

> 'Energy and persistence alters all things.'
>
> **BENJAMIN FRANKLIN, 'THE FIRST AMERICAN'**

 ## MEET MARK

When I started coaching Mark, he seemed worn out and dispirited. He had spent the previous eight months setting up his own company. What initially had seemed so exciting now seemed a chore. He was getting bogged down in all the things running a company involves – areas such as accounting and marketing. He had become used to the luxuries of being an employee where there is a whole department of support colleagues, but, when you are on your own, you even have to fix the printer yourself.

We examined activities in a typical day and how Mark was feeling about each one. We found that actually he had lost sight of his initial idea and the plan that had so excited him to strike out on his own was now very hazy to him. As a result, he had no enthusiasm and felt drained of energy.

Energy is having your motivation, your attention and your attitude all aligned and somehow this had all become skewed for Mark and he felt lethargic.

It became vital for Mark to focus on actions he could take to boost his energy and get him back on track, including the basics of diet and exercise, as well as everyday coping strategies to feel more in control. These can seem like small things but they can make a dramatic difference.

This involved consciously focusing on jobs and reminding himself of his talents and why he wanted to work for himself. Purposely he slowed down to concentrate and consider whether the job in hand was worth expending energy on. He started taking regular breaks to clear his mind and, importantly, kept hydrated. It is very easy to neglect ourselves when very busy.

Mark is now feeling much more positive and his spark has returned. His enthusiasm about his work is back and he has landed a high-value project, which also will allow him to recruit two new colleagues, an assistant and a project manager.

Observe people at work who you consider to have high energy:

- Who do you know who has high energy at work, who gets pleasure from doing something well?
- What range of work activities do you see this person involved in?
- What have they accomplished in the last few years?
- What signs do you have that they gain enjoyment from the things they are involved in?
- Which activities are they involved in, that they seem to enjoy and do effortlessly?
- Which activities in work do you wish you had more motivation to do?

Use these questions to observe yourself:

- What things do you put effort into that are not really important?
- What are the financial perks and incentives you need in order to do your best?

- In which activities have you lost interest or given up on recently?
- Is anything you have stopped doing in the past a problem for you now?
- Do you work best under pressure or without pressure?
- Which part of the day do you look forward to the most? Which parts of the day do you dislike the most?
- What do these two contrasts mean to you in your everyday work? What do they contribute?
- When you go about your day-to-day activities, what aspects make you feel fulfilled?
- Where do you spend most of your energy? On the fulfilling activities, or the others?

Improving your energy

Working through the tools in this section will help you to make a shift in your energy at work. There are three tools included here:

- energy audit;
- values audit;
- SWAN.

1. Energy audit

Make a list of all the things that give you energy and all the things that drain you. Write these in two columns:

What gives me energy:	What drains me:

Then cluster these and group them under separate headings, so that you end up with no more than 10 in each column.

Think of specific actions you can take to increase your energy and remove some of the drains on your energy.

 You can download an example of a completed energy audit from the web resources.

Examples of possible strategies to mitigate energy drain, depletion of energy or decision fatigue include:

- Eat fresh fruit (natural sugars) rather than sugary foods in the day.

- Consciously focus on the effect of water bringing calm.

- Slow down.

- Stay in control by reminding yourself of your gifts, talents, skills and ability to cope effectively with day-to-day demands and pressures.

- Clear your physical workspace.

- Build in short breaks – for example, when having a snack, actively focus on this being a break from what you are doing.

- Continue to tune into your heart when you start a meeting or travel to see a client.

2. Values audit

Complete this for clarity and focus.

Which work values are important for you? Select five you think are the most important. Identify how you can use these proactively in your future interactions to connect with people when you are networking/social-ising, etc.

Examples include:

- achievement
- challenge
- creativity
- ecology/environment

- flexibility
- helping others
- meaningful work
- productivity

- profitability
- service
- teamwork
- work/life balance

In the table below, list your three key values and then write a definition for each. Then describe what the value looks like when implemented – i.e. in action. When you are living out this value what do you do? Also note any values that need more emphasis in your work.

Value	My definition	What it looks like in action	Does this value need more emphasis at work?

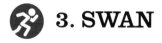 ## 3. SWAN

The word SWAN is one you will find useful to keep a continuous track on wherever you are in your job. Please list these four specific aspects of your current work life, and try to review this list regularly to keep it current.

Strengths – what are your strengths both in terms of emotional resilience and your other job skills (technical, leadership, technology related)?

Weaknesses – what are your weaknesses both in terms of emotional resilience and your other job skills?

Ambitions – looking forward three to five years, and even further, what would you absolutely love to achieve?

Necessities – what is your current need in terms of income, lifestyle and relationships that are important for you to achieve at work?

Chapter **13**

Thriving

'The best moments usually occur when a person's body or mind is stretched to its limits in a voluntary effort to accomplish something difficult and worthwhile.'

MIHALY CSIKSZENTMIHALYI, AUTHOR AND HUNGARIAN PSYCHOLOGY PROFESSOR

This chapter will give you:

- an insight into how thriving is a result of the skills of emotional resilience as well as the essentials being in place;

- three tools for being able to thrive at work including defining your criteria for doing your best work, deciding how to learn more about your career interests, and creating a living legacy plan.

Thriving
Organising yourself to be effective under pressure

How does one keep vitality and maintain high performance at the same time? Is happiness mutually exclusive from being highly effective at your job? I think you can aspire to both if you are emotionally resilient and able to handle what comes up on a daily basis at work.

Having worked alongside people who are very good at thriving, no matter how challenging their job, I have noticed that these people have two tools in their lives – a clear plan for what is important to them in their work, and everyday routines for handling work and home priorities. I call this a 'living legacy' that you create every day in the context of other things in life that are important to you.

The work you started in Chapter 12 Energy now continues with building a solid time plan and a set of aspirations so that how you spend your time matches what you want. Having a solid plan in this way is not typical and I find that it determines who is able to sustain their work versus who is not. The plan needs to reflect clearly the values you wrote in your values audit in Chapter 12.

Whilst change is now a given at work, our challenge is to consider that change is for our own good and to find ways around the obstacles presented to us. This relies on us trusting that any changes are positively intentioned, which is hard to do but can make a very big positive impact when we are trying to sustain a high level of performance at work. This can be difficult to do at a time when an unpopular change is occurring at work (for example, a restructuring of tasks, which reduces our work and therefore our income), but perhaps a key question might be:

'How might this change actually help me in the long term?' or 'What could I learn from this change?' In this example, it could be that the reduced tasks actually give you the flexibility to do something else that could be even more fulfilling and linked with something that you want to learn.

How effectively you adapt to new environments, conditions and challenges will depend on how solidly you set yourself up for success. This chapter is about exactly that – the small things that matter to you and how to put them in place for the longer term.

The combination of your plan and being flexible is what matters for your emotional resilience.

Thriving involves having an effective way to handle the inevitable pressure and stress of work and determines how effective you are in balancing work and life. The goal is to handle pressure calmly and effectively through having good coping mechanisms. More often than not, if you are good at controlling your emotions (see **Part 1 The Essentials**), you will be more likely to be able to tackle stress.

If you look at the definition you will see that thriving means: 'to keep up vitality under pressure; to maintain high performance'. For this, I believe you need a passion and belief in what you are doing.

 ## MEET NICK

I met Nick and his wife after he had completed an overnight bike ride for a breast cancer charity. Both his wife Nina and her best friend had been diagnosed with cancer around the same time, but were doing well. However, it brought into sharp focus a different life problem of serious health risks that affect so many people and create emotional turmoil.

Nick looked to what he could do to raise money and awareness for the charity. He had not been on a bike since being a teenager and, now in his forties, it felt like a new and daunting experience. He found it tough to complete the first event but now he trains regularly and has finished several long-distance races to raise funds and get the charity noticed.

Signing up for the next race immediately puts him under pressure, but the passion to make a difference and raise funds sustains him when his energy and the weather are out to test him.

He believes so much in what he is doing that it both sustains and motivates him when the going gets tough.

 Observe people at work who you consider to have strong skills in sustaining high performance:

- Who do you know that is good at staying on top of high-pressure situations, without losing their cool?

- What steps does this person take to control their anxiety and to face difficult situations? (Ask them if you are not sure what their strategies are.)

- Which of these steps or actions do you wish you could demonstrate more often?

- Who do you know who is able to change their opinion, when all the facts and evidence are presented to them or when a full and complete discussion has been held?

- Which type of adaptability would you most like to work on in yourself:
  - Your ability/desire to make an important change in your work life?
  - Your reaction to new initiatives?
  - Changes to your work pattern that do not go smoothly?

Use these questions to observe yourself:

- What are the triggers for stress in your life?

- How can you anticipate them earlier?

- Are you a good self-observer of when stress starts to take hold?

- What is the pattern to your stress? (Time of day, situations, people, when tired?)

- Where in your work are you adaptable and where are you relatively less flexible?

- When you are under pressure, do you become more or less flexible?

- What messages do you hear from other people that are related to flexibility in the face of change? (For example, is there anyone close to you who, typically, says, 'You always say that', 'You don't change, do you?', 'Why don't you try something new?')

- How do you plan your day? Do you place more emphasis on the activities that give you a sense of fulfilment and meaning, or do you do things in the order in which they present themselves to you?

Improve your thriving

This section includes four activities to help you develop the ability to thrive in your workplace.

1. Criteria for my best work

This tool involves writing down a set of job criteria for your ideal or dream job. Hopefully, your current job is not too far away from it! Please adapt the example below to suit your type of work.

Complete column 1 first and then assess your current job against the criteria using column 2.

Essential – this aspect of your job is very important to you, without it you are not really interested in having a particular job.

Desirable – this aspect of your job is something you would like ideally, but it is not a 'deal breaker' if you do not find it in a job. If you do have it, you prefer it to another job without it.

The key is to distinguish **what is essential** and **what is desirable** (but not essential) in each aspect of your job. Create your own criteria using the example overleaf.

If the match with your current role is below 70 per cent, then it is likely that a portion of your energy will be drained by what does not work for you in your job and you will be feeling unfulfilled. Sometimes it is not possible to change jobs right now but, what we can do is pay more attention to the things that work well for us. This activity on defining criteria is one that many people find extremely helpful in understanding where their energy is consistent with what they really want.

Column 1: **Write the essential and desirable features of your job here.** Write these now so that you can use them to reflect on your current job and how well matched it is to your ideal.	Column 2: **Think about your current job and how well it matches each feature in Column 1.** **Give a % from 0 to 100%.** Do this after completing column 1 Key Questions.
What words would you use to describe what is important to you in five areas of your job?	% match of current role against essentials and desirables
1. Content of role What does the job ideally involve you doing? Write down the key tasks you enjoy. Decide what is *essential* and what is *desirable*. **Example** **Essential:** Global, multi-community Leadership Not repetitive, diverse (variety) Expert in something Mentoring – a few clearly defined relationships and also helping many more junior people **Desirable:** Link to Asia Leading a large team	

2. Meaning of role
Who and what does your job impact?
Decide what is essential and what is desirable.

Example
Essential:
Making people's lives better
Business and world problems

Desirable:
Walking the world stage

3. Logistics
What are the important practical considerations relating to where and how you work?
Decide what is essential and what is desirable.

Example
Essential:
Travel to work – 20 mins x 3 times a week
65% home-based
Have breakfast
Evening meals at home – 4 evenings out of 7

Desirable:
Travel to work – 20 mins x 5 times a week

▶

4. Impact on life

Thinking about your time outside of work, what is important for you in your home life?
Decide what is essential and what is desirable.

Example
Essential:

Source of friendships outside work
At least once a week commitment to a hobby
Six weeks holiday possible
Income of £X,000 per year
Safe location to live in
Able to retire at 65

Desirable:
Easy travel to extended family in X location during work week

5. Relationships

Thinking about relationships at work, what is important to you?
Decide what is essential and what is desirable.

EXAMPLE
Essential:

Opportunities to build community of friends at work
Partner is excited about my work

Desirable:
Best friend at work
Regular social activities at work

6. Preparation for future
Thinking about this job in the context of your wider life goals, how does it help you with what is likely to happen next?
Decide what is essential and what is desirable

Example
Essential:
Taking on a future job in Asia or Europe is possible after this one
Constantly learning technical skills

Desirable:
Job involves Asia or Europe

7. Any other criteria?
Write any other essential or desirable criteria.

Total match with current role
(divide the % in column 2, by the number of items you listed, then convert this number to a percentage)

2. Career interests

This tool involves making a list of all the things that interest you in your job so that you can learn more about them.

Include on this list all of the things that really interest you. Then acquire more knowledge of these things (via reading, courses, media, talking to others with similar interests, etc.) and make a serious effort to get more involved in them. Another way to get into this activity is to imagine that you have only three months longer to work – what are all the things you would love to learn about?

Things to learn about:

To make this happen you may wish to:

- schedule time each week for self-development, for example, mastering a skill you already have;

- experiment with new tasks at work to discover what suits you and your personality best;

- explore: you may discover that you have hidden interests and talents that can give you a great deal of gratification and satisfaction;

- make a list of short-term and long-term goals in pursuing and accomplishing new areas of development, skill and talent;

- share your interests with other colleagues – tell people what interests you.

3. Time planning – 168 hours/ 6 areas of life

'Retirement is when you stop living at work and start working at living.'

ANON

This tool involves creating a solid plan for your life goals (including your work), which can become your living legacy. One area that is particularly useful for emotional resilience is to be clear about how you want to spend your time (or life). Research confirms that writing about your life goals is aligned with enhanced well-being (King, 2001). Using time well is a preventative strategy for making it easier to manage and deal with emotional situations as they arise. It also means that your weekly use of time reflects what you really want.

This is an exercise that helps you to be very clear about how you use your time, and what is important to you. I have found that people who work through this activity are more likely to be able to maintain good relationships with others and live both a work life and a home life that is in tune with what they really want.

How it works

Use the categories of time below to help you work towards a balanced life where all your needs are met.

CATEGORIES OF TIME FOR LIVING

Intellectual: this includes all the time you wish to spend learning about things that interest you, so that you can grow yourself, for example, interests, hobbies, new skills, new competences, new areas of expertise.

Financial/material: this includes all the time you spend adding to your financial security and dealing with financial priorities, for example, savings, investments, projects.

Spiritual: this includes all the time you spend nurturing yourself spiritually, for example, prayer, inner peace, meditation, giving back to the community.

Physical: this includes all the time you spend helping yourself to be physically on top form, for example, exercise, recreation, sleep, nutrition, personal grooming, personal care.

Social: this includes all the time you spend with other people, for example, family, friends, neighbours, community, holidays, fun.

Career: this includes all the time you spend working, including travelling time.

It is useful to visualise these six categories of time as forming a lifebelt, something that holds your life intact. The design of lifebelts is very specific, divided into sections, and it floats you to safety, even if one or more sections are slightly depressed.

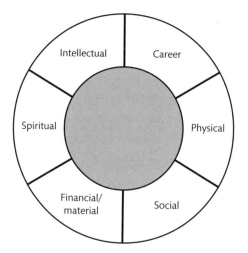

Step 1. Using the two blank lifebelts below, draw in each of the six categories of time listed above, adjusting the size of each section to reflect how you spend your time **now** and, ideally, how you would like to spend your time, in an **ideal** world. Note that, when drawn and completed, the size of each section should reflect your actual views about your life.

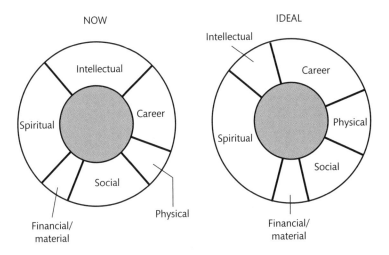

NOW
Intellectual
Career
Social
Physical
Financial/
material
Spiritual

IDEAL
Intellectual
Career
Physical
Social
Financial/
material
Spiritual

Step 2. Now list the specific weekly activities that would provide you with a highly fulfilling, satisfying life within each of the six categories of time listed above in your ideal lifebelt.

Allocate a total time per week to each of the six categories consistent with the proportions you have drawn on the lifebelts.

Total time per week for all 6 areas = 168 hours.

Be specific about the activities you want to do in each of the six categories of time. Make the activities really specific. For instance, if under the social category you wish to be a caring, consistent friend, you might phone your best friend a certain number of times each week; to be a great father may involve you doing certain activities with each of your children every weekend. Remember, there is a total of 168 hours in the week. Try to avoid the temptation to plan for more than 168 hours! See some examples below.

Area of life	Activities	Resources (people, time, energy required)
Physical	**Examples:** Jogging Long walk Sleep	3 hours 2 hours 49 hours **54 hours**
Social	**Examples:** Weekly date night with partner Conversation with friends (in person) Meeting a work friend for catch up Quality time with family	3 hours 2 hours 1 hour 9 hours **15 hours**
Career	**Examples:** Team meetings Key customer meetings Quiet time Admin time Travelling Computer work	1 hours 18 hours 3 hours 1 hour 20 hours 15 hours **58 hours**

Spiritual	**Examples:** Contribution to community Alone time	2 hours 2.5 hours **4.5 hours**
Intellectual	**Examples:** Reading outside core work Learning a new skill	3 hours 1 hour **4 hours**
Financial/material	**Examples:** Paying bills Dealing with personal savings	2 hours 2 hours **4 hours**
Other List here anything else not covered by the previous six sections.	**Examples:** Getting ready each morning/personal hygiene Eating meals Watching TV/reading Domestic chores – cleaning, cooking, shopping, etc.	7 hours 9 hours 6 hours 6.5 hours **28.5 hours**
Total		**168 hours**

Someone I met many years ago hung a sign on his office door:

> 'Every week, I spend:
> 38 hours with my partner
> 15 hours with my family
> 16 hours going out with friends
> 54 hours sleeping and keeping fit
> Therefore I have 35 hours to come to work'

Step 3. Now go back to the six categories of time and write a best outcome (living legacy statement) for each of the six categories. Write it as if you have already achieved it and write it in the third person. The goal can be very simple and short – for example under physical, 'He was fit and healthy even in his eighties'; under social, 'He was a caring and consistent friend and colleague and a great parent', and under job, 'He did great work and enjoyed technology'. They can also be longer – 'He was physically in shape throughout his life, always looking more youthful than his peers. He had more energy and vitality to do the things he enjoyed.'

Living legacy goals	
Intellectual	Financial/material
Spiritual	Physical
Social	Job

Step 4. The final step is to identify the key milestones from now for achieving each living legacy goal. For example, the current step in achieving the physical living legacy goal mentioned earlier of being fit and healthy might be to:

start a regular exercise programme – 3 times a week for 30 minutes;

eat healthily at least half of the time, progressing to 75 per cent of the time at the end of the first six months;

join a running club.

 You can download an Excel file and a worked example from the web resources.

4. Time management tips

With the living legacy format clear, it is going to be useful to decide how to be careful or more regulated about your use of time. Here are a variety of examples to help you to achieve efficiency and effectiveness in your work and home life. Try to implement at least three tips straight away.

1. Understand yourself better

- Keep your living legacy objectives close to hand and visible either on your phone, tablet or on your wall at home.

- Think in terms of results to achieve, rather than work to be done.

- Work smarter not harder – spend more time on the important, less on the urgent.

- Start the day off with an enjoyable job – this achievement will set you up for the rest of the day.

- Remember – you will feel better having completed a job (possibly tired and frustrated, if you have not).

2. Plan the day

- Plan tomorrow, tonight.

- List all tasks (both work and home).

- Prioritise all jobs.

- Estimate times for each job.

- Commit yourself to particular times in the day for the jobs.

- Divide larger projects into smaller, more manageable tasks and concentrate only on those tasks that truly require your attention at that moment.

- Get to know your high energy time and do the most important things then.

- Leave part of the day unplanned to deal with crises.

- Include one step from an important project in each day's plan.

- Plan a quiet time or non-interruptible time each day.

- Work in longer cycles – plan weekly, monthly, quarterly.

3. **Reduce crises**

- Avoid leaving things to the last minute.
- Keep your main living legacy goals in mind – do not get side-tracked by urgent, but relatively unimportant, things.
- Remember, things often take longer than you think – allow for this in planning.
- Encourage your colleagues to help you to stay on track with work commitments.
- Use the problem-solving tools in this book for handling problems when they occur.

4. **Work meetings**

- Ask yourself, 'Is the meeting really necessary?' (Remember what you could be doing instead.)
- Have a detailed agenda, with objectives and a timetable for all meetings – however informal.
- Start on time, keep to time and finish on time.
- Use creative visual aids to stimulate thought and discussion. Write down key points if you have no visual aids.
- Do not allow interruptions from outside the meeting.
- Restrict notes you write to any agreed actions (named) and deadlines.

5. **Interruptions**

- An 'open door' policy is an attitude – not to be interpreted literally for every minute of the day.
- Say 'No' (nicely!) more often.
- Be more honest with timewasters.
- Get away from the office for important, detailed, creative work.

6. **'Managing' the need to be always available**

- Introduce periods of time when you are not going to be disturbed.
- Set aside times for email/internet use and avoid being available all the time.
- Develop the skill of closing a phone call, so that you can focus on your priorities: 'I need to go in two minutes...'

- Try to get right away from the phone/computer/people when you need quiet time.

7. Keep a clear workspace

- Only papers relating to your current task should be there.
- Tell others that you want to keep your workspace tidy, if others share it.
- Clear your workspace completely each night.
- Spend a whole day throwing out all papers and clutter.

8. Delegate (for team leaders)

- When colleagues/staff bring you problems at least expect possible solutions from them.
- Delegate **both** responsibility **and** authority.
- Agree on a process for checking that a job has been done.
- Ensure your team members are clear about their objectives and review them often.
- Set and expect high standards of work and performance.
- Stop upward delegation.
- Regularly ask for feedback on your style of working.

9. Self care

- Rely more on others to help you confirm/reality check whether your commitments are achievable.
- Do not commit yourself too early – check that you have the resources/time to do it.
- Make sure you do not help other people to manage their demands, at some cost to you.
- Give yourself as much value as you do others.
- Anticipate more, let go of unimportant things, learn the difference between **urgent** and **important** and spend more time on **important**.
- Be prepared to ask for help sooner rather than later.
- Have a plan for exercise and relaxation built into your week.

- Laugh more – laughter releases health-promoting chemicals.
- Play more! Recreation means recreate.
- Take your well-earned holidays.

10. Managing stress and pressure

- Be aware of how you feel in stressful situations.
- Try to understand how these situations develop and what makes them so stressful for you.
- Believe in your ability to handle and successfully overcome stressful situations when they occur.
- Learn deep-breathing techniques.
- Learn how to relax.
- Practise visualisation in advance of stressful situations.
- Use your social support system to help manage stress.
- Make a plan to renew your body, mind and spirit.
- Focus on the things within your realm of control. Do not sweat the small stuff.
- Maintain perspective; learn to step back; learn to say 'no'.
- Smile often.

11. Handling change (these actions will save you time)

- Change something in your daily routine frequently so that you have the experience of new routines and new perspectives. For example: a different route, find a new hobby or group that involves joining other people.
- Do not be afraid of change – accept it as an opportunity to learn new things and grow.
- Practise relaxation techniques to calm your anxiety when you are in uncomfortable, ambiguous situations.
- Try to maintain mental adaptability when others are expressing ideas that you are not comfortable with. Listen and try to learn more about them.
- Allow your mind to open to new thoughts or ways of doing things.
- Continuously engage yourself in learning something new.

Chapter **14**

Connection

'A machine has value only as it produces more than it consumes – so check your value to the community.'

MARTIN H. FISCHER, GERMAN PHYSICIAN AND WRITER

This chapter will give you:

- an insight into how connection with others is a result of the skills of emotional resilience as well as the essentials being in place;

- two tools to track your key relationships – a dependency diagram and a stakeholder analysis.

Connection
Building relationships through personal interactions

Connection is the positive impact of your social skills, how you develop the relationships that are important to your work success. When you have strong relationships at work you are socially sensitive, adaptable, and perceptive around the needs of your stakeholders. This can make you very skilled at negotiating, brokering deals, and interacting with others to get your job done.

With the **Skills** and **Essentials** we covered earlier, you are likely to be in control of your emotions and the manner in which you express them to others, which enables you to function confidently in social situations at work – meetings, networking events and informal gatherings. Where people do not have good connections, typically they feel anxious in unfamiliar settings because they are unsure about how to behave. They find it difficult to express themselves clearly and have a small circle of acquaintances. They are known for their limited interpersonal skills.

The Center for Creative Leadership (in Greensboro, North Carolina, USA) studied the reasons for leaders losing track of their careers and found that it was never to do with cognitive ability – the two most common traits of those who failed were rigidity and poor relationships.

This chapter focuses on two tools – a dependency diagram for charting out your important relationships at work and also a stakeholder analysis for deciding who are the people at work you most need to have a solid relationship with, because your success depends on the quality of these relationships.

'People with trustworthy relationships and personal support systems at work and with friends and family are more able to cope with stress and organisations more likely to hold up in a crisis.'

PETER JOHNSON-LENZ, AMERICAN CYBER PIONEER

Being able to connect with people can be vital to how successful you are at work and creating strong relationships with colleagues, stakeholders or clients is an important skill we should all practise.

MEET TIBAULT

When I first met Tibault, he had been offered a promotion but, much as he wanted it, he was considering turning it down. It would mean attending a lot of regional meetings with people he did not know, more client contact and presenting, plus various high-level social functions. He was worried about his ability to connect with people but knew that he had to make a good impression to gain and retain business.

As part of taking a solid look at this problem, we decided that he would shadow two well-established networkers whose full-time jobs are to network with local businesses, large and small, and then use the learning to improve himself. I suggested that he observe them closely and note how they present themselves, how they stand, what they say and how they engage a new contact in conversation. The idea was to observe someone who was good at connecting with others (a tool that is used throughout this book). Many people do not use the learning opportunities that are right in front of them.

Although reluctant at first, through doing this Tibault learnt tips and strategies to approach new people and give the impression of confidence, even if he was not feeling it. Eventually, he started to relax and, with some breathing techniques, the idea of building business connections became less daunting and he was able to take on his promotion with less trepidation.

Observe people at work who you consider to have strong skills in connection:

- Who do you know who is a good citizen, someone who is genuinely helpful and more interested in others than in themselves?
- What do they actually do to help other people?
- How do they show the extent to which they care for and respect other people?
- Which charity or community activities are they involved in outside of their work context?

Use these questions to observe yourself:

- At work, what support do you offer people outside of your job role and immediate area of responsibility?
- What opportunities exist in your daily life to do something altruistic that typically you ignore?
- What small things do people do for you that make a difference to your work life and give you a feeling that someone else is looking out for you?

Improving your connection

Working through the tools in this section will help you to make a longer-term shift in your connection with others. There are two tools included here for application at work:

- dependency diagram;
- stakeholder analysis.

1. Dependency diagram

Start by drawing a circle in the middle of the page and write your name in it.

Start by listing all the people you interact with at work. You may wish to write these randomly, scattered on the page around the circle. List as many people as possible.

Identify on whom you are dependent for what kinds of things. Use the following letters to identify the specific type of help you receive from others.

P = practical help

A = advice

C = companionship

E = emotional support

I = intellectual connection

H = honest feedback

O = other (list the type of support)

Reflect on the degree of dependence you have – for example, people on whom you are the most dependent might be closest to the circle and people on the edge of the page might be the most distant.

Once you have this drawn, identify how you could become either more or less dependent. Which things from this list would you prefer to be able to provide for yourself independently of others? Which types of support would you like more of and who could provide this?

To build an emotional connection with people, it is useful to contact them first and to increase the frequency of communication with them if there is mutual interest in forming a closer working relationship – sometimes it is useful to start with more emails or more calls to them. At other times you might plan more face-to-face meetings.

> **'The only relationships in this world that have ever been worthwhile and enduring have been those in which one person could trust another.'**
>
> **SAMUEL SMILES, SOCIAL REFORMER**

2. Stakeholder analysis

List all your key stakeholders. A stakeholder is anyone who can judge your success in your job. Your stakeholders might include people at the same level as well. These people might already be on your dependency diagram or they may include an entirely new set of people.

Decide how important and how strong your relationship is with each stakeholder.

You might wish to consider each stakeholder on qualities of TRUST that you learned about earlier (see Chapter 11 Dialogue), on a scale of 0 to 10. Remember that each quality needs to exist both ways for it to be present in the relationship.

Think about the step change you desire in the relationship and what would be the ideal frequency and nature of contact – this could be a wide range of things from a call, to a regular email, to a regular update, to less frequent meetings or group meetings. The whole activity is designed to help you to be proactive about what type of relationship you want to build.

You can download a template from the web resources.

Stakeholder name and position	How important? (low - medium - high)	How strong is the relationship now? (low - medium - high)	Step change you desire in the relationship	Ideal frequency and nature of contact if relationship is strong	First step to initiate closer contact: call, conversation or email? By when?

Chapter 15

Influence

'When a team outgrows individual performance and learns team confidence, excellence becomes a reality.'

JOE PATERNO, AMERICAN FOOTBALL COACH

This chapter will give you:

- an insight into how the five passions of life may get in the way of influencing others;

- two tools for staying on track with what you are delivering to your stakeholders – a self-assessment on your influence at work and learning how to influence.

Influence
Leading and managing relationships with stakeholders, colleagues and team members

The way we conduct ourselves in teams and groups in our jobs will influence both how others perceive us and how well we get on in our jobs. Some of the typical behaviours we want to be able to display at work are:

- standing up for our rights and beliefs;

- being able to take charge in certain situations;

- being a natural leader, even in challenging circumstances/firm authority;

- being self-reliant;

- taking the initiative and assuming control of events;

- influencing and directing others with confidence;

- encouraging debate, whilst having the firmness to end it and move on;

- being resilient in the face of negative feedback;

- standing up to criticism;

- being prepared to challenge others;

- not being afraid to enforce standards, push people for results and confront poor performance;

- being trusted by others.

👥 MEET JULIA

Things are not always straightforward at work and, when I met Julia, the company she worked for was going through a very bad spell with redundancies imminent. Rather than sit back and see what happened, Julia was proactive in taking control of events and trying to ensure the team stayed together.

Influence is about how to exercise power over what happens in a positive way. One member of the team needed to be dismissed but, with careful discussions and a well-prepared argument, all staff were retained, albeit on reduced hours. Julia was able to influence the entire management through a well-prepared statement, clear arguments and agreement from her team members. Her peers and key stakeholders were convinced that it was a well-thought-through proposal and financially manageable. The result was that everyone remained employed.

So, the question is how do you influence others and how do you exercise power over what happens in a positive way? The whole series of recent breaches of trust and misjudgements by politicians, business people and various other people in authority roles has made me wonder about how to avoid falling into the trap of getting carried away with power. The power that I am referring to in this chapter is impact and influence rather than unwieldy power.

> **'In the midst of difficulties, opportunities exist.'**
>
> **ALBERT EINSTEIN, GERMAN PHYSICIST AND PHILOSOPHER OF SCIENCE**

To stay on the right side of power, I believe we need to understand the five wrongdoings (or passions of the mind, as they are sometimes referred to in spiritual teachings) that can get us into trouble. They are natural perversions of human nature until we can learn to control ourselves to keep our side of the street clean at all times – they are vanity, lust, anger, greed and attachment. In moderation, we can be effective with these at work but, if any of these are out of control or if we have too much of a good thing with any of these, it will affect how we conduct ourselves in groups, as well as how we are perceived.

Vanity or ego – there is nothing wrong with having good self-worth but, when you start to think you are better than other people and you start to communicate this to other people, it becomes unmanageable and, potentially, damaging at work.

Lust – desiring love or attention from someone inappropriately, or excessive food or drink, can cloud the mind and dull our awareness of emotion.

Anger – there are times when you feel you have been wronged and you need to stand up for yourself. But, when you object too much, it becomes anger, criticism and gossip.

Greed – of course you want things and need certain things to work effectively, but everything needs to be in moderation. When we cross the line into greed we are out of control.

Attachment – when you have your job, your home life, your family and your belongings, you get to a stage when you like them too much and you become possessive and do not like to let go of them.

At work, you need to be on guard continually against these five passions of the mind, as they can slip in and steal our attention away from emotional resilience and get us locked into a negative trap with serious consequences. They are also useful to keep in mind to use our intuition when a situation does not seem right.

We want to be sure not to take these five passions of the mind with us on our resilience journey. The actions that often can help us to keep these passions at bay are the opposites: forgiveness, tolerance, contentment, discrimination, detachment and humility.

The end goal is well summarised in one of the 700 verses of the *Bhagavad Gita*, the universally renowned jewel of India's spiritual wisdom. Spoken by Lord Krishna, to His intimate disciple Arjuna, the following verse provides a concise goal for modern-day resilience:

> **'One who is not disturbed in mind even amidst the threefold miseries or elated when there is happiness, and who is free from attachment, fear and anger, is called a sage of steady mind who is not at all angry even when his attempts are**

unsuccessful. Success or no success he is always steady in his determination.'

PRABHUPADA (1983) CHAPTER 2, VERSE 56

Improving your influence

The two tools in this section are a self-assessment on your influence and a tip on staying firm on our promises at work.

1. The three Ps: politics, patience and presence

Given the five passions of the mind described earlier, the checklist below is designed to help you review some of the content in earlier chapters and decide which behaviours you need to keep in check.

Place a tick next to each behaviour that you think you are susceptible of displaying.

These 20 characteristics have been adapted from the list of annoying habits of leaders in the book *What Got You Here Won't Get You There* by Marshall Goldsmith (2008). These characteristics are derived from his work with leaders and there is a strong overlap with the six essentials from the framework for Developing Emotional Resilience®. All of the annoying habits are related to either sharing too much information/emotion or not sharing enough. Hopefully, they will serve as a useful reminder to keep working on the essentials.

Absence of balanced self-worth:

☐ Adding too much value: the overwhelming desire to add our penny's worth to every discussion.

☐ An excessive need to be me: exalting our faults as virtues simply because they are who we are.

- [ ] Claiming credit that we do not deserve: the most annoying way to overestimate our contribution to any success.

- [ ] Passing the buck: the need to blame everyone but ourselves.

- [ ] Refusing to express regret: the inability to take responsibility for our actions, admit we are wrong, or recognise how our actions affect others.

- [ ] Winning too much: the need to win at all costs and in all situations.

Absence of balanced self-control:

- [ ] Passing judgement: the need to rate others and impose our standards on them.

- [ ] Speaking when angry: using emotional volatility as a management tool.

- [ ] Telling the world how smart we are: the need to show people we are smarter than they think we are.

Absence of balanced mood:

- [ ] Making destructive comments: the needless sarcasm and cutting remarks that we think make us witty.

- [ ] Negativity or, 'Let me explain why that won't work': the need to share our negative thoughts, even when we are not asked.

Absence of balanced empathy:

- [ ] Not listening: the most passive-aggressive form of disrespect for colleagues.

- [ ] Punishing the messenger: the misguided need to attack the innocent who are usually only trying to help us.

- [ ] Starting with 'No', 'But', 'However': the overuse of these negative qualifiers, which secretly communicate to everyone, 'I'm right and you're wrong.'

Absence of balanced understanding:

☐ Clinging to the past: the need to deflect blame away from ourselves and onto events and people from our past; a subset of blaming everyone else.

Absence of balanced caring:

☐ Failing to express gratitude: the most basic form of bad manners.

☐ Failing to give proper recognition: the inability to give praise and reward.

☐ Making excuses: the need to reposition our annoying behaviour as a permanent fixture, so people excuse us for it.

☐ Playing favourites: failing to see that we are treating someone unfairly.

☐ Withholding information: the refusal to share information in order to maintain an advantage over others.

🏃 2. Six honest serving men

This final activity is focused on six key questions to ask yourself in order to stay on track with what you have promised to deliver (and is memorialised by Rudyard Kipling in his poem, 'Six honest serving-men'). Before you make a decision or take a course of action, run through the five Ws and one H:

- **What** is the outcome/deliverable/agreement?

- **Why** did we/I decide this?

- **When** is the deadline?

- **Where** is the project going to happen?

- **Who** is involved and what are their roles?

- **How** are we going to get there?

Use this checklist in meetings, on the phone and when you plan things with other colleagues. It can help as part of using your energy in the right way and being sure that you are going to be influential with your actions. It helps you to engage your skill in being effective.

You can also use this as a situation check, to set the scene of a meeting, to pause and recap on progress, or to help other people explain to you where things are up to. Ask them to answer these questions for you.

FINAL WORDS

I would like to leave you with a few words about the real-world importance of emotional resilience.

I believe that today, in workplaces everywhere, we have a conundrum that only we can resolve.

We have built organisations through a desire for doing something good (whether to serve the community, advocate for a cause or build the wealth of its owners). Whatever the arena of work you are in, most organisations seem to run a big risk by continuing to ignore the role of emotion in achieving success for and in their organisation.

Programmes aimed at building emotional skills have been at the periphery of real work and, at times, have been considered to be soft and only for non-commercial human resources professionals. Widespread attempts to build these into education or health at large have not yet been effectively carried out. Many business leaders do not consider the role of emotion until a problem occurs.

These trends must change.

Emotion matters for success. The research evidence is now at a point where we can no longer ignore the central role of emotion in work productivity, health, personal effectiveness and team performance.

The unaddressed dysfunctional patterns we observe at work have taken their toll on individuals and teams. At work we see unmet needs continually played out, often in dramatic ways. Those managers and employers who have insight into the role of emotion in our work lives are able to use this information to make effective decisions and to support high performance that feels good and is sustainable.

We can aspire to build organisations where emotion is not only valued, but welcomed as a way to meet the needs of employees and make full use of employee talent. We can cultivate work cultures where people of all levels accept and use their feelings as a source of information, motivation and connection. This is the only way to be at our best.

If you are a senior leader, helping your people to be emotionally resilient in the face of pressure, stresses and challenges is not only a good thing to do, it is vitally important if you want your team or organisation to achieve success at the highest levels – no matter how you define success.

The concept of emotional resilience presents an opportunity for people to have available to them all of their resources: personal, psychological and social, and to use these resources to help them build and sustain high performance and personal well-being. These are not mutually exclusive – people can and should achieve both at the same time.

Enlightened organisations already recognise that emotion affects the performance of individuals and teams.

If you are a decision maker or someone who can influence the widespread up-skilling of work populations in these skills, I have a few points to leave you with.

I have focused this book on emotional resilience as a series of coping strategies, based on the combination of work on self and work in interactions with other people. Whether or not an individual at work will choose to learn these will be a largely self-directed matter, unless a person's employer or all organisations in a sector choose to invest in training in these skills and behaviours.

If you care about the performance of the people in your organisation, then these skills ideally would be considered as foundational rather than a luxury for a chosen few. Emotional resilience distinguishes the people who perform and cope with stress effectively from those who just get by, one project or one day at a time.

It is time to bring the skills and practices of emotional resilience into a much wider arena to influence the changes we desire in the workplace and further afield.

As Charles Darwin discovered, 'It is not the strongest of the species that survives, nor the most intelligent. It is the one that is the most adaptable to change.'

We now know that emotional resilience provides the foundation for human adaptability.

What did you think of this book?

We're really keen to hear from you about this book, so that we can make our publishing even better.

Please log on to the following website and leave us your feedback.

It will only take a few minutes and your thoughts are invaluable to us.

www.pearsoned.co.uk/bookfeedback

REFERENCES

Introduction

Chartered Institute of Personnel and Development (2011) 'Developing resilience: an evidence-based guide for practitioners'. Accessed online on 25 September 2014.

Ekman, P. (2003) '16 enjoyable emotions', *Emotion Researcher*, 18, 6–7.

Elfenbein, H.A. (2007) '7 Emotion in Organizations', *The Academy of Management Annals*, 1 (1), 315–386.

Erikson, E.H. (1950) *Childhood and Society*. New York: Norton.

Chapter 1: Self-worth

Ainsworth, M.D.S. and Bowlby, J. (1991) 'An ethological approach to personality development', *American Psychologist*, 46, 331–341.

Csikszentmihalyi, M. (1997) *Flow: The Psychology of Optimal Experience*. New York: Harper Perennial Modern Classics.

James, W. (1890) *Principles of Psychology*. New York: Henry Holt.

Klontz, T. Seminar presentation delivered at Onsite Workshops, Nashville, USA.

Liu, S.Y., Wrosch, C., Miller, G.E. and Pruessner, J.C. (2014) 'Self-esteem change and diurnal cortisol secretion in older adulthood', *Psychoneuroendocrinology*, 41 (111).

Chapter 2: Self-control

Mischel, W. (2014) *The Marshmallow Test: Mastering Self-Control*. London: Bantam Press.

Chapter 3: Mood

Danner, D.D., Snowdon, D.A. and Friesen, W.V. (2001) 'Positive emotions in early life and longevity: findings from the nun study', *Journal of Personality and Social Psychology*, 80, 804–813.

Fredrickson, B.L. (2001) 'The role of positive emotions in positive psychology: the broaden-and-build theory of positive emotions', *American Psychologist: Special Issue*, 56 (3), 218–226.

Pychyl, T.A. (2013) *Solving the Procrastination Puzzle: A Concise Guide to Strategies for Change*. Carleton University, Ottawa, Canada.

Rottenberg, J. (2014) *The Depths*. AZ: Basic Books.

Tomasulo, D. (2010) 'Proof positive: Can heaven help us? The nun study – afterlife', Psych Central. Accessed on 26 September 2014, from http://psychcentral.com/blog/archives/2010/10/27/proof-positive-can-heaven-help-us-the-nun-study-afterlife/.

Chapter 4: Empathy

Flury, J. and Ickes, W. (2006) 'Emotional intelligence and empathic accuracy' in Ciarrochi, J., Forgas, J. and Mayer, J. (Eds) *Emotional Intelligence in Everyday Life: A Scientific Enquiry* (2nd edn), 140–165. New York: Psychology Press.

Scott, B.A. Colquitt, J.A., Paddock, E.L. and Judge, T.A. (2010) 'A Daily Investigation of the Role of Manager Empathy on Employee Well-Being', *Organizational Behavior and Human Decision Processes*, November 2010, Vol. 113 (2), 127–140.

Chapter 5: Understanding

Druskat, V.U. and Wolff, S.B. (2015) 'Team Emotional Competence', working paper. University of New Hampshire, Durham, NH, USA.

Fiske, S.T. (2004). *Social Beings: A Core Motives Approach to Social Psychology*. Hoboken, NJ: John Wiley & Sons.

Fonagy, P., Gergely, G., Jurist, E. et al. (2002) *Affect Regulation, Mentalization and the Development of the Self*. New York: Other Press.

Chapter 6: Caring

Druskat, V.U. and Wolff, S.B. (2015) 'Team Emotional Competence', working paper. University of New Hampshire, Durham, NH, USA.

Emmons, R.A. and Crumpler, C.A. (2000) 'Gratitude as a human strength: Appraising the evidence', *Journal of Social & Clinical Psychology*, 19, 56–69.

Ryback, D. (1998) *Putting Emotional Intelligence to Work: Successful Leadership is More Than IQ*. Boston: Butterwork-Heinemann.

Vanette, D. and Cameron, K.S. (2009) 'Implementing positive organizational scholarship at Prudential', Ross School of Business, William Davidson Institute.

Chapter 7: Shifting

Carter, R. (1999) *Mapping the Mind*. London: University of California Press.

Chapter 8: Problem solving

Hanson, R. (2009) *Buddha's Brain: The Practical Neuroscience of Happiness, Love, and Wisdom*. Oakland, CA: New Harbinger Publications.

Pert, C.B. (1997) *The Molecules of Emotions: Why You Feel The Way You Feel*. London: Simon & Schuster.

Simon, H.A. (1967) 'Motivational and emotional controls of cognition', *Psychological Review*, 74 (1), 29–39.

Chapter 9: Expressing

Brown, B. (2012) *Daring Greatly: How the Courage to Be Vulnerable Transforms the Way We Live, Love, Parent, and Lead.* New York: Gotham.

Brown, B. (2010) *The Gifts of Imperfection: Let Go of Who You Think You're Supposed to Be and Embrace Who You Are.* Center City, MN: Hazelden.

Brown, B. (2013) *The Power of Vulnerability: Teachings on Authenticity, Connection and Courage.* Audio CD. Sounds True Inc.

Carr, P. and Walton, G. (2014) 'Cues of working together fuel intrinsic motivation', *Journal of Experimental Psychology.*

University of California – Los Angeles (22 June 2007) 'Putting feelings into words produces therapeutic effects in the brain', *Science Daily.* Retrieved on 2 November 2014 from www.sciencedaily.com/releases/2007/06/070622090727.htm.

Chapter 10: Group empathy

Pert, C.B. (1997) *The Molecules of Emotions: Why You Feel The Way You Feel.* London: Simon & Schuster.

Rice, C.L. (1999) 'A quantitative study of emotional intelligence and its impact on team performance', unpublished Masters thesis. Malibu, California: Pepperdine University.

Chapter 11: Dialogue

Hanson, R. (2009) *Buddha's Brain: The Practical Neuroscience of Happiness, Love, and Wisdom.* Oakland, CA: New Harbinger Publications.

Chapter 12: Energy

Hanson, R. (2009) *Buddha's Brain: The Practical Neuroscience of Happiness, Love, and Wisdom.* Oakland, CA: New Harbinger Publications.

Tierney, J. (2011) 'Do you suffer from decision fatigue?', *NY Times Magazine.* 17 August 2011. Accessed on 26 September 2011 from http://www.

nytimes.com/2011/08/21/magazine/do-you-suffer-from-decision-fatigue.html?pagewanted=all&_r=3&.

Tierney, J. and Baumeister, R.F. (2011) *Willpower: Rediscovering the Greatest Human Strength*. London: Penguin Books.

Chapter 13: Thriving

King, L.A. (2001) 'The health benefits of writing about life goals', *Personality and Social Psychology Bulletin*, 27, 798–807.

Chapter 15: Influence

Goldsmith, M. with Mark Reiter (2008) *What Got You Here Won't Get You There: How Successful People Become Even More Successful – Discover The 20 Workplace Habits You Need to Break*. London: Profile Books.

BIBLIOGRAPHY

Ainsworth, M.D.S. and Bell, S.M. (1970) 'Attachment, exploration, and separation: Illustrated by the behavior of one-year-olds in a strange situation', *Child Development*, 41, 49–67.

Aldwin, C., *et al.* (2014) Center for Healthy Aging Research at Oregon State University. Research update accessed on 26 September 2014 from http://health.oregonstate.edu/synergies/2014/even-small-stressors-may-harmful-mens-health-new-osu-research-shows/

Cacioppo, J.T. and Patrick, W. (2008) *Loneliness: Human Nature and the Need for Social Connection*. New York: Norton.

Cacioppo, J.T., Reis, H.T. and Zautra, A.J. (2011) 'Social resilience: The value of social fitness with an application to the military', *American Psychologist*, 66 (1): 43–51.

Damasio, A. (1994) *Descartes' Error: Emotion, Reason and the Human Brain*. New York: Gusset, Putnum.

Erikson, E.H. (1950) *Childhood and Society*. New York: Norton.

Fonagy, P., Gergely, G., Jurist, E.L. and Target, M. (2002) *Affect Regulation, Mentalisation and the Development of the Self*. New York: Other Press.

Gorelick C., Milton, N. and April, K. (2004) *Performance Through Learning: Knowledge Management in Practice*. Burlington, MA: Elsevier Butterworth-Heinemann.

Hebb, D.O. (1961) 'Distinctive features of learning in the higher animal' in Delafresnaye, J.F. (Ed.) *Brain Mechanisms and Learning*. London: Oxford University Press.

Huy, Q.N. (1999) 'Emotional capability, emotional intelligence, and radical change', *Academy of Management Review*, 24 (2): 325–345.

Loerbroks, A., Bosch, J.A., Douwes, J., *et al.* 'Job insecurity is associated with adult asthma in Germany during Europe's recent economic crisis: a prospective cohort study', *Journal of Epidemiology and Community Health*. Published online 22 September 2014.

Maddi, S.R. and Khoshaba, D.M. (2005) *Resilience at Work: How to Succeed No Matter What Life Throws at You*. New York: AMACOM.

Mental Health Foundation (2010) 'The lonely society?' www.mentalhealth. org.uk/campaigns/loneliness-and-mental-health/. Accessed on 25 September 2014.

Office for National Statistics (2012) 'Divorce rates data, 1858 to now: how has it changed?' http://www.theguardian.com/news/datablog/2010/jan/28/divorce-rates-marriage-ons – accessed on 25 September 2014.

Office for National Statistics (2013) 'Measuring national well-being, older people and loneliness', http://www.ons.gov.uk/ons/rel/wellbeing/measuring-national-well-being/older-people-and-loneliness/index.html and http://www.ons.gov.uk/ons/dcp171766_304939.pdf. http://news.bbc.co.uk/1/hi/7898510.stm. Accessed on 25 September 2014.

Perry, P. (2012) *How to Stay Sane: The School of Life*. UK: Macmillan.

Relate (2014) http://www.relate.org.uk/blog/2014/8/12/4-5-are-happy-couples-1-10-have-no-close-friends-our-new-study-lifts-lid-uks-relationships. Accessed on 25 September 2014.

Siebert (2005) *The Resiliency Advantage: Master Change, Thrive Under Pressure, and Bounce Back from Setbacks*. San Francisco, CA: Berrett-Koehler Publishers.

Tugade, M. and Fredrickson, B.L. (2004) 'Resilient individuals use positive emotions to bounce back from negative emotional experiences', *Journal of Personality and Social Psychology*, 86, 320–333.

Waugh, C.E. and Larkin, G.R. (2003) 'What good are positive emotions in crises? A prospective study of resilience and emotions following the terrorist attacks on the United States on September 11th, 2001', *Journal of Personality and Social Psychology*, 84, 365–376.

WEB RESOURCES

 All resources can be accessed at:
eiworld.org/emotional resilience.

Free resources/downloads

Introduction

Business case for emotional resilience

Worksheet for emotional resilience self-reflection

Part 1: Essentials

Highs and lows exercise on self-worth

Setting healthy boundaries and creating healthy balance between competing areas of work life and life in general

Affirmations template and worked example

Who am I poster template

Atmospheres video link

Mood cost-benefit analysis template

Book list – self-worth

Quotes on self-worth

Neutralising mood – examples

Part 2: Skills

TED talk on empathy

Resources on co-dependency

Emotion barometer – example

Team emotional intelligence survey framework and articles

Building trust template for activity

High life/low life activity example

Recording of body scan sequences

Suggestions of music to play whilst recalling moments of pure enjoyment

TED talks on vulnerability and shame

Part 3: Results

List of useful supplements

Energy audit – example

Living legacy – worked examples and templates

Stakeholder analysis

If you experience any problems with the downloads, please email emotionalresilience@eiworld.org.

ADDITIONAL RESOURCES

These additional resources are proprietary and have a charge associated with them.

Information about these resources can be accessed at **eiworld.org/ emotionalresilience.**

- Emotional intelligence surveys

- Team emotional intelligence survey

- Emotional resilience – self survey

- Emotional resilience – 360 degree survey

- Executive coaching delivered anytime, anywhere

- Development of high-performing teams

- Emotional resilience coaching

- Up-skilling internal coaches in emotional resilience

For more information on these additional resources, please email info@ eiworld.org.

YOUR FEEDBACK

For me, there is nothing more motivating than to see a person or a team working at their full potential, and for this impact to be noticeable by everyone around them at work and in their home lives.

Please let me know when you start to make changes that are noticed by others. The greatest gift in my work is to be in dialogue with people who use this material to make a change in their work lives.

Please give me your feedback on the content of this book:

E: gbharwaney@eiworld.org
W: eiworld.org

EMOTIONAL RESILIENCE E-LEARNING

Do you want to roll out the ideas in this book to a larger population through your company e-learning platform?

The author is collaborating with Pearson to make available modules for delivery via e-learning for application in organisational contexts.

For any queries, please contact:

E: gbharwaney@eiworld.org
W: eiworld.org

INDEX

Priority topics for emotional resilience

Colour a circle each time you circle one of the characteristics of 'negative impact'. Notice where you feel 'heavy' from the circles.

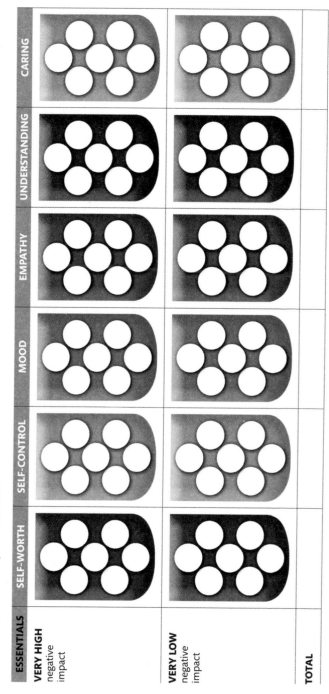

ESSENTIALS	SELF-WORTH	SELF-CONTROL	MOOD	EMPATHY	UNDERSTANDING	CARING
VERY HIGH negative impact						
VERY LOW negative impact						
TOTAL						